SITUA

MW01118143

"By using a time-tested formula, Mary pinpoints strategic thinking needs in each area of an organization as she helps them learn to effectively prioritize, assess risks, and create long-term strategies for success."

— **David M.R. Covey**, CEO of SMCOV, Coauthor of *Trap Tales: Outsmarting the 7 Hidden Obstacles to Success.*

"Buck the trend and make a lasting and effective change with this book! Every leader should have it."

— **Marshall Goldsmith**, New York Times #1 best selling author of *Triggers, Mojo,* and *What Got You Here Won't Get You There.*

"*Situational Mindsets* teaches leaders that they don't need an MBA. They need to stay curious, ask the right questions, and read this book! The six mindsets helped me see new possibilities for my own business as well as empowering my executive coaching clients to make positive changes. I predict *Situational Mindsets* will become a classic leadership book for the ages."

— **Dr. Marcia Reynolds**, author of *The Discomfort Zone: How Leaders Turn Difficult Conversations into Breakthroughs.*

"Count on Mary Lippitt to see the world of leadership through a refreshingly new angle and bring her immense wisdom to its thoughtful practice. *Situational Mindsets* will open your eyes, clarify your perspective, and sharpen your influence in bringing the best of who you are to what you do."

— **Chip R. Bell**, author of *Managers as Mentors: Building Partnerships for Learning.*

"What the "just in time" is to inventory management, Mary Lippitt's Situational Mindsets concept will be to whole-of-business management. This is an eminently practical blueprint for business leadership in an era of relentless transformation."

> — **Alan Axelrod**, author of *The Disruptors: 50 People Who Changed the World*, and *Profiles in Audacity: Great Decisions and How They Were Made.*

"Challenge is the opportunity for greatness, and in *Situational Mindsets* by Mary Lippitt, you will discover the mindsets that leaders must have to navigate current challenges and turn them into exciting opportunities. It's a breakthrough work with a unique perspective that will make you think differently about how you think. And, you'll want to return to it regularly for its wise counsel on what you can do to have more of the brilliant and less of the blunder. I highly recommend it."

> — **Jim Kouzes**, coauthor of the award-winning *The Leadership Challenge* and Executive Fellow of Center for Innovation and Entrepreneurship, Leavey School of Business, Santa Clara University.

"Lippitt's approach is in my tool kit under the heading of "elegant process and solutions." It collapses several dynamics into a streamlined result—the silver bullet that leaders embrace."

> — **Dr. Virginia Bianco Mathis**, Managing Partner, Strategic Performance Group; Professor and Director, School of Business and Technology, Marymount University.

"*Situational Mindsets* offers a valuable tool for dealing with complexity and change using insights across the organization. In our dynamic environment, we must critically assess our realities and gain active support for execution.

This book provides a checklist roadmap for engagement and results."

— **Kimo Kippen**, Founder Aloha Learning Advisors, LLC and Former Chief Learning Officer for Hilton.

"I have used Dr. Lippitt's work in my graduate leadership course at the University of South Florida for several years now. She has the amazing ability to evaluate an organization's current position and see the potential opportunities and downfalls of their current operations. Each time the students walk away with a tangible tool that is entrenched in theory to help them be more effective in the workplace. Executive and budding leaders alike have seen the value in using this comprehensive system."

— **Dr. Doreen MacAuley**, Professor of Management at the University of South Florida.

"Mary's original ideas will stretch your thinking and push you toward becoming a better leader who embraces the challenges of uncertainty, the promises of opportunity, and the impediments of complexity. Delve into this book; it is a must read from a thought leader who has devoted her career to helping others learn to lead and achieve results."

— **Elaine Biech**, author *The Business of Consulting*, editor *The ASTD Leadership Handbook* and founder of ebb associates inc.

"Mary Lippitt presents in actionable detail the six situational mindsets that every leader will need throughout a task or project's lifecycle to achieve success. *Situational Mindsets* is a book you will be glad you read and that you will find yourself repeatedly referring to."

— **Hile Rutledge**, President/Principal Consultant, OKA (Otto Kroeger Associates).

"Figuring out what is going on is always a challenge in the complex world of organizations. As work itself becomes more complex, multifaceted, and collaborative, the need to do good situational analysis becomes ever more important, especially in teams and projects that cut across hierarchical lines. This book offers an excellent template for differentiating the requirements of different kinds of situations and should, therefore, be useful to all managers and employees.

> — **Edgar H. Schein**, Professor Emeritus, MIT Sloan School of Management, Co-author of *Humble Leadership: The Power of Relationships, Openness, and Trust* (2018).

"*Situational Mindsets* targets today's critical leadership dilemma—how to handle thorny problems, complexity and risk. This book reveals no-nonsense insights on how to develop wise and agile leaders."

> — **Daniel J. Doyle**, Chief Human Resources Officer, Beall's, Inc.

SITUATIONAL MINDSETS

Targeting What Matters
When It Matters

Mary Lippitt

Foreword by **David Covey**

Published by Enterprise Management Limited, 4531 Roanoak Way, Palm Harbor, FL 34685, 727-946-4200

Library of Congress Cataloging-in-Publication Control Number
2 0 1 9 9 0 8 3 6 4

ISBN 9 7 8 0 9 7 1 5 9 0 7 3 1

Printed in the United States of America

TidePods is a registered trademark of Proctor & Gamble. 737 Max 8 is a registered trademark of The Boeing Company. IPod and IPad are registered trademarks of Apple Inc.

FIRST EDITION First printing 2019

To those who inquire, engage, and analyze to achieve goals.

Contents

Foreword

I am honored to write this foreword on behalf of my good friend and trusted colleague, Dr. Mary Lippitt. Mary is not only an award-winning speaker, author, and leadership consultant, and she is also a pioneer in the realm of change.

I believe we can all agree that change is inevitable. And we often don't mind as long as it doesn't happen to us. We fear change for a myriad of reasons but primarily because it forces us out of the warm little cocoon where we have felt safe and comfortable for a long time. This cocoon may not provide all that we need, and it may feel a bit too snug, but it is all we know. Thus, we heartily embrace our old habits, our assumptions, and our thinking about life and the people with whom we share relationships.

Yet after a while, we may begin to feel like something is missing. Like a thunderstorm coming over the horizon, we see the signs before it starts to rain. Albert Einstein once said, "The world as we have created it is a process of our thinking. It cannot be changed without changing our thinking." So enters this book and Dr. Mary Lippitt.

Leaders must make choices. Amid the tumultuous climate of today's global market, Mary's comprehensive approach to leadership focuses on helping both organizations and individuals identify specific decisions and judgments that may be hindering their long-term growth and prosperity. In simpler terms, she helps these leaders find what needs to be changed and shows them why and how to do it. By using a time-tested formula, Mary pinpoints strategic thinking needs in each area of an organization as she helps them learn to effectively prioritize, assess risks, and create long-term strategies for success.

Mary offers six "success mindsets," which, when utilized properly, teach leaders how to check the pulse of an organization's current workplace conditions and allow them to respond to the dynamic global climate. These six success mindsets are Inventing, Catalyzing, Developing, Performing, Protecting, and Challenging — each one crucial to the function and success of an organization. Let Mary show you why.

Reading this brilliant book was both a pleasure and a gift. It has not only helped me to analyze my own leadership tendencies and skills, but it caused me to take notice of the changes I need to make within my own organization to gain a competitive advantage in today's world. Mary's input is invaluable because she is firmly results-driven yet also personable and attentive to the process.

Her book is not some quick-fix solution of putting a bandage on systemic problems only to see them resurface later on. Her context-analysis approach to organizational leadership has proven to be vital and sound. Mary is a dedicated and passionate professional. She brings creativity and warmth to whatever she touches.

The author, C.S. Lewis once wrote, "We can't be afraid of change. You may feel very secure in the pond that you are in, but if you never venture out of it, you will never know that there is such a thing as an ocean, a sea. Holding onto something that is good for you now, maybe the very reason why you don't have something better."

Let's strive for something better.

— **David M.R. Covey**, CEO of SMCOV, Coauthor of *Trap Tales: Outsmarting the 7 Hidden Obstacles to Success.*

Introduction

"The dogmas of the quiet past, are inadequate to the stormy present. The occasion is piled high with difficulty, and we must rise — with the occasion. As our case is new, so we must think anew, and act anew."

— ***Abraham Lincoln***

Sailors read the wind, sea, and compass to set their sails. Generals study the terrain, supplies, and weather to craft their strategies. However, attention to context is missing in most organizations. *Situational Mindsets* offers a unique model to effectively scan the environment, weigh alternatives, and address growing complexity and changing realities.

We collect and juggle multiple situational variables in our personal lives. Consider how we drive. Studies indicate drivers adjust the steering wheel and check their mirrors every five to ten seconds in response to traffic congestion, lane changes, road conditions, and slow-moving vehicles. Driving demands vigilance and awareness. Taking our eyes off the road—to answer a call or grab a drink—is dangerous.

Leaders continually face rapidly changing challenges. We cannot duplicate another firm's strategy or that of a celebrity CEO—or operate in a void—and expect to flourish. We must recognize our current realities, evaluate alternatives, and prioritize action. Making the right call for the right results requires situational awareness and mental agility.

While leaders' characteristics, styles, and competencies remain critical, we need help to recognize and leverage fluid external conditions. Situational awareness must augment self-awareness. Leaders need a framework to critically collect and analyze conditions. Although we may want to tackle multiple alternatives, we cannot. Limited time, resources, and talent mean we have to make choices. Collecting and evaluating multiple variables is essential to making smart decisions for the short and long term.

As leaders, we may hope for a steady state, assured that we know what to do, when to do it, and what resources are required to produce the desired results. However, we do not control events. They control us. But we can control and leverage our responses to our benefit. In order to do that, we need to rigorously assess what we are facing, what our options are, and what takes priority at this moment. We cannot be blinded by outdated assumptions and operating practices if we want to capture opportunities and control risk. Understanding current realities, employing critical thinking, and pivoting deliver the outcomes we seek.

Situational awareness prevails in sports more than it does in organizations. Golfers study course contours, weather conditions, and ball placements before they select a club. They would not use a putter on the driving tee or a wood on the green. Golfers adjust to where they are and what they confront.

Football coaches read the opposition's defensive formation and adjust accordingly. They cannot run the same play every down and expect to score. Successful quarterbacks are those who can read a situation and detect the smart play. Context counts when it comes to reading the golf course, reading the play, and reading an organization.

Continual change is maddening, but limiting ourselves to existing practices and thinking means we miss opportunities. Whether we are aspiring or experienced leaders, the status quo provides little prospect for reward. As financial planners remind us, past success does not guarantee future results. We must adapt because change is probable, pervasive, and problematic.

Military leaders deploying tactics from a past war cannot expect to win a new one. The British Redcoats were ill-prepared for a guerrilla war in the colonies. Strategies, weapons, and the landscape were different.

Organizations, also, must adjust to changing tides. Toys-R-Us, Sears, Blackberry, Kodak, Blockbuster, Yahoo, Commodore, MySpace, RadioShack, Borders, Palm, and Circuit City stuck with stationary business models for too long. The ain't-broke-don't-fix-it mentality is as foolish to adopt as the mindless change-for-the-sake-of-change strategy. Some people seize on one position, but conviction and history cannot substitute for accuracy or deliver success. Static and limited outlooks invite risk.

Abraham Maslow observed that when you only have a hammer, everything appears to be a nail. Indeed, such a limited view is mistaken, but so is the other extreme of attempting to focus on everything. Not everything warrants immediate attention. Judgment is vital.

Getting it right requires up-to-date information and timely action. Entering a market late reduces margins and the probability of success.[1] However, if we wait until we have every bit of information before deciding to act, we will be paralyzed into inaction.

Critical thinking involves extracting information from data, detecting patterns among many signals, and identifying implications from mountains of data. Mining insights requires discipline rather than an advanced degree, elevated IQ, or lofty title. We prove that every day as we set priorities and allocate our personal assets based on what we consider crucial.

Yet a few managers still assume that few people can decipher trends and leverage change. This outdated assumption limits engagement, innovation, and opportunity. For example, frontline employees have firsthand knowledge, and they make smart decisions when leaders give them the opportunity.

Decision makers at all levels can effectively scan their environment, extract key insights, discover alternatives, evaluate risks, and target key issues. But these require structure. Working memory is limited to juggling only three or four things at one time,[2] well short of the number of key variables we face. Therefore, we need a discipline to collect and gauge the glut of information. Many CEOs cite the need for enhanced critical thinking, innovation, and strategic perspective but do not provide the necessary tools. This book presents a practical checklist to use when confronting complexity and ambiguity.

Leaders do not need to know it all, but we must ask about it all. Penetrating queries shed light on complex issues. We do not lack data or talent; we lack a system for widening our vantage points to see all there is to see. If we miss key aspects, we can pay a high price.

Consider Tide PODS, one of Proctor & Gamble's most innovative products. Launched in 2012, the brightly colored packets captured one-fifth of the laundry-detergent market by 2018. Eight deaths and approximately nine thousand poisonings resulted from the PODS, as well. Could these have been foreseen? Many would argue it was possible, given that young children are attracted to vivid colors, particularly when they can hold an object. Failure to consider the design impacted the brand and the bottom line.

Likewise, Boeing mistakenly decided to classify as an extra feature the Maneuvering Characteristics Augmentation System (MCAS) software package that would override potential sensor malfunctions on the 737 MAX 8 airplane. Given that the plane cost over $120 million,[3] a 5 percent up-charge for safety was short-sighted, especially when combined with reduced pilot training. Two major crashes later, those choices have cost the firm billions of dollars.[4]

These two examples were not black-swan events. They were foreseeable and unacceptable, but not unique. Both firms have outstanding leadership and expertise. What they lacked in these examples was rigorous situational awareness.

Situational Mindsets outlines how to obtain information, discover the best answer, influence others, and deliver results. It presents a Situational Mindsets Checklist tool to organize key data for fresh insights and critical assessment. Questions foster engagement, spur creativity, and gain alignment. While we wish we could shape circumstances to meet our needs, in reality, we must adjust to our conditions.

To introduce this framework, the book begins with a quasi-case history about Kate Hollander, a composite of many leaders I have worked with. She is starting her position as vice president of sales at a struggling printing company. Sales are lagging, and finger-pointing, mistrust, and micromanagement reign. She uses Situational Mindsets to resuscitate sales despite a team that doubts her abilities. Regardless of these obstacles, she also builds collaboration and promotes strategic planning using Mindsets.

While the firm and names are fictional, the storyline is not. It reflects my research and more than thirty years of consulting experience with critical thinking and mental agility. This framework is easy to apply. It quickly transforms teams, and it produces results.

After Kate's scenario, the final chapters connect her story to the practice of Situational Mindsets. These chapters describe how to use Mindsets to see more than initially meets the eye and deliver results.

Whether you are a team member, team leader, or

business owner, this book will improve your ability to capture opportunities, build commitment, recognize pitfalls, and deliver tangible benefits. My sincere wish is that you tailor and use the Situational Mindsets Checklist for your circumstances.

I welcome your observations and comments, so please feel free to share them with me at mlippitt@enteprisemgt.com. I wish you incredible success.

PART

ONE

Kate Hollander and Transition

1

A New Start

Kirkuk, Iraq. Under fire—distant artillery flashes and shell bursts punctuated by the *pop-pop-pop-pop* of AK-47s. The wounded would be trucked in any minute.

Six years she had been here—Sergeant First Class Kathryn A. Hollander, Sixty-Eight Whiskey (68W) combat medic. The noise, detonations, dangers—terrifying to untrained civilians—were just another day at the office for her. Kate set to work—steady, selective, skilled. From one to the next, she moved with dedication, performing exactly as she had been trained.

Being the right person at the right place with the right equipment when things got hot in combat instilled skills and a confidence Kate had never known. Napoleon had been able to take in a battlefield at a glance, evaluating all its opportunities and dangers, identifying what was immediately important to attack or defend and what could wait: *coup d'oeil*. But as a medic, Kate had learned a different *coup d'oeil*: triaging the wounded and rapidly deciding the order of treatment most likely to save lives. Head wound but alert—*Priority*. Lower leg missing, bleeding out—*Emergency*. No pulse here. Wailing over there. She scanned the wounded, prioritized critical needs, and gave instructions to worried mates to hold IVs. In short order, all the injured were prepped for transport to the hospital. Everyone was going to make it. *Emergency. Priority. Non-urgent in the queue.* Amidst the tumult, she assessed then aided the wounded one after the other in the order of their urgency.

A sound blared in her ear ... incoming? She turned around to see what was happening.

•

Kate opened her eyes. As usual, she woke up before the alarm. The dream, while stunningly real, was reassuring. *You have done this. You* can *do this.* The dream had extended rather than disrupted her sleep. She had gone to bed keyed up about applying for a job as vice president of sales at Davis Printing Company. It had taken her a while to doze off, but she would still take her morning run before heading to the interview.

She pulled her red hair up into a ponytail, put on her sweats and ski vest, and completed her circuit in the nearby hills as the sun rose. Later, showered, dressed, and coifed, she walked to the full-length mirror standing in the corner —conservative make-up, hair smooth, and a dark-gray suit pants pressed, and one-inch heels under her five-foot-nine frame. No camos today.

After breakfast, she donned her suit jacket and coat, then drove from her Airbnb rental in Golden, Colorado. She loved that this little town lying at the foot of the Rockies was founded during the Pike's Peak Gold Rush of 1859.

The plant was twenty minutes away in central Denver. Enough time to enjoy the snow-covered foothills that offered both soothing and invigorating vistas, from expanses of rolling ground to angular, jutting rock formations. The environment was certainly a contrast to the flat desert terrain of her three tours in Iraq. She looked forward to a permanent residence after years in the army. This may be the place and opportunity.

As Kate drove, she reflected on her previous jobs and training. While she had been an exceptional athlete in high school—excelling at volleyball and track—she had been an indifferent student who enrolled in a community college after graduation. Her father, an internist, hoped she would pursue a bachelor's degree and maybe enroll in medical school. But after two years and a general associate's degree, Kate went to work as a sales rep for MedSurgicals, a fast-growing medical device manufacturer outside of Phoenix. She thought her father would be happy she was connected to the field of medicine.

Kate proved to be a natural at selling and advanced to sales manager. Despite a heavy workload, she continued her education. She majored in business, studying at night and on weekends until she earned her bachelor's degree. At the same time, she moved up to Director of Sales, reporting directly to the COO.

Then came the terrorist attacks of September 11, 2001. Overcome with outrage, grief, and patriotism, Kate decided she would not be a passive victim, nor would she let her country be a victim. She would take charge of her future—and America's—by joining the United States Army. She knew exactly what she wanted to be and enlisted as a combat medic, following her dad who had served in a field hospital during the Vietnam War. He paled at the news but managed to tell her how proud he was. Probably thought this would start *her* medical career.

During her third deployment to Iraq, she was posted in Kirkuk with a forward-area medical company supporting an infantry-combat team. When the shooting started, and the wounded were brought in, she went into full combat-medic role. Captain Richard Price headed one of the combat team. His tour of duty ended before hers, but they stayed in touch.

When Kate separated from the service, she knew she couldn't get her medical-supply job back. And she didn't want to. She wanted a new challenge. After she emailed Richard that she planned to return stateside, he responded with an interesting proposal. He had joined a small printing firm in his hometown of Denver. He started as a production supervisor, but the owner, Tom Davis, recognized his ability to think on his feet and deliver results. Skills that the army had polished. Richard became vice president of operations, which was great because he was now married and planning a family. He asked her to consider joining the firm in Sales.

In a follow-up call, he said, "Kate, I'll give it to you straight. I moved up fast not just because Tom Davis liked me but because this place needed leaders. Still does, particularly in the Sales Department. Those folks are nice, but they need someone to put a fire in their bellies. They're drifting, even with falling sales."

"Sounds like something's not right there."

"Exactly. What with digital technology and the Net, the industry's changing. Suddenly, we're up against a load of online printers and more-efficient presses. Now, Tom built this company and still wins business through sheer charisma, but he refuses to keep up with the times, let alone get us ahead of the curve."

Kate wanted a challenge, but she did not want to run into a stone wall either.

"I get as far as I can, but then Tom shuts me down. Besides, I don't have sales credibility. I need an ally, Kate, and Sales desperately needs an overhaul. I know leadership, and you nailed it in Iraq. You can make a difference here with your sales experience and leadership. I want to set up an interview for you with Tom for the VP of Sales position."

Kate was flattered, but she had been away from sales for *six years*! She hesitated, but Richard *knew* about her sales hiatus. And he had seen what she was capable of in Kirkuk. That was more demanding and complicated than any sales job. Maybe she should take the interview for the VP slot.

Her corporate training kicked in along with her confidence and the action-oriented Catalyzing Mindset she relied on when she was in sales management. When confronted with the choice of "lead, follow, or get out of the way," she wanted to lead. While she didn't have any printing knowledge, she could read customers and quickly learn the industry. She could transfer what she knew about selling medical devices into selling printing. After reinventing herself as a combat medic, making the leap from selling in one industry to another would be a sure bet. However, she balanced her thinking with a careful analysis using the Challenging Mindset to gauge future risks as well as opportunities. Fueled by careful review and her desire to plan her future, she decided the potential rewards significantly outweighed potential problems.

Forward was the only reasonable direction. Besides, she had aced interviews before. "Richard, that would be great! Give me a day to dust off my résumé."

And dust it she had, highlighting the success of her sales team at MedSurgicals. Having prepared in every way possible, she was now heading to the interview. The more she thought about the prospect of helping Davis Printing succeed the more excited she became.

•

Arriving for her interview, Kate pulled into the parking lot. According to Richard, Davis Printing occupied a former lighting factory, a single early-twentieth-century red-brick building that contained both the offices and plant. The neighborhood was in the first throes of gentrification. Across the street was the SoHo restaurant, a local restaurant on the verge of becoming trendy with a fusion menu, full bar, and oriental art. Nobody would call Davis Printing trendy. Anyway, Kate wasn't looking for Silicon

Valley chic. She wanted challenge and opportunity.

Kate turned the tarnished brass door handle and entered Davis Printing. Richard was waiting for her in the dull gray lobby. His sandy-brown hair could still pass military inspection—it was as short as the nap of the lobby's seafoam-green carpet—but he had grown a closely trimmed beard. She couldn't be sure, but home cooking seemed to have grown on him too. A bit of desert tan remained on his face and neck above the collar of his blue dress shirt.

Richard stepped past the receptionist's desk, hand extended. "Kate, so good to see you again." His brown eyes creased above his genuine smile.

The corners of Kate's mouth lifted as she firmly shook his hand. "You too. Thank you for arranging this."

The receptionist stopped inserting papers into envelopes and gave her a quick ruby-lipped smile, as well as a once over, then reached for the phone on her desk, which had started ringing. "Good morning, Davis Printing, this is Angela, how-may-I-help-you?" She pushed her glasses up with one manicured finger, then picked up her pen and started jotting on a note.

"Let me take you to Tom." Richard pointed toward the hallway on her left. As he escorted her down the hall, noise bounced off the concrete floor, along with a distinctive smell of ink solvents. He stopped at the door of a small office where a brown-haired middle-aged woman sat rigidly at an immaculate desk.

Without entering, he said, "Kate, this is Debbie Conrad, our office manager."

"Kate Hollander," Debbie said. "Yes, glad to see you. Tom's waiting for you."

Richard led Kate into the next room. "Here she is, the most dynamic soldier I've ever served with."

Tom Davis rose from his seat behind a varnished mahogany behemoth that instantly reminded her of Resolute, the desk in the Oval Office. He walked around the desk, closing two open drawers as he came. "Welcome to Davis Printing." Tom was just a few inches taller than she, enough to meet her eye-to-eye. "A pleasure to meet you, Kate." He extended his hand, and a broad smile spread across his face.

It seemed to be the practiced smile of someone who had great presence and enjoyed nothing more than being in his own office and in command. With his thick mane of silver-white hair, he could pass as a president of the United States, except that his desk was heaped haphazardly with papers and folders. Every picture she had ever seen of the Oval Office showed a clean desk, no matter who was president.

Kate noticed that a huge faded black-and-white photo of the building covered the wall behind his desk. The picture displayed a line of men cutting the ribbon for a farm-implement store, which was adorned with bunting. The building's inauguration was clearly decades earlier from the look of the cars parked nearby. The outside of the building looked the same, with only a different name over the door. The building had stood the test of time.

Tom followed her gaze, then pointed to the picture. "She may not win an architectural award, but she has good bones." He obviously adored the place, in spite of its age. According to Richard, the company was Tom's baby, and he loved it, except for falling sales.

"Richard thinks the world of you, Kate"—Tom motioned for them to sit in the chairs before his desk—"and I value his recommendation. But I have to add that I've been in the printing industry for over thirty years and value experience—*industry* experience—and frankly, remain concerned about your lack of printing experience. However, I would be happy to be proved wrong by an immediate boost in sales and customer satisfaction." Finally, he sat in his own chair.

Such a challenge could have torpedoed the whole interview. But instead of forming a defensive posture, Kate held his eyes. She was confident in her abilities and willing to meet high expectations. She could deliver on the bottom line *and* dispel his doubts.

"I understand your concerns, Tom, and I respect that it will take industry knowledge to succeed. However, I'm a quick study. If I wasn't sure of that, I wouldn't be here. I wouldn't want to waste your time, or mine. I can get up to speed shortly to lead a successful sales team. If you hire me, I can deliver fresh perspectives, new opportunities, and significant growth."

Tom nodded and smiled. "That's good to hear."

The interview settled into predictable details. In the end, Kate knew she had not magically dismissed all of his reservations, but he repeated a few times how much confidence he placed in Richard's recommendation. And since they would need to work together, their strong relationship was a plus. Despite his preference for someone with printing-industry experience, he could not afford to wait to fill this key position. Sales needed leadership *now.* He called the next day and offered her the position.

She knew that Tom would support sales initiatives. Given Richard's intel, she also knew that the challenges she would face. She accepted the job. Crazy? No crazier than what Hernán Cortés did in the sixteenth century when he reached Mexico—and promptly scuttled his ships so the conquistadors would have no choice but to conquer the Aztecs. She was all in.

•

Friends congratulated Kate on leaping from army NCO to corporate vice president, but some expressed concern at how swiftly she bought a house *before* her first day on the job with a company that was hardly a standout. Kate listened. She understood. However, she had done a careful analysis. Her sales-management training had stressed the importance of collecting and evaluating information from six points of view. She used that framework when deciding to purchase the house. It was basically a business decision, so she considered:

- **Inventing:** recognizing what she needed to update in the home, including technology and security

- **Catalyzing:** understanding the housing market and acting quickly when opportunities surfaced

- **Developing:** analyzing structure, local traffic patterns, availability, and regulations

- **Performing:** calculating short- and long-term costs and negotiating the sale effectively

- **Protecting:** meeting her neighbors and walking the neighborhood

- **Challenging:** testing her basic assumptions and planning for her future

Employing these Mindsets, she examined things from all perspectives to make a wise choice. Just as she had while evaluating the VP position.

•

As Kate entered the lobby on her first workday, she was pleased when Angela told her that Tom had asked to be notified when she arrived. Even though she was early, he promptly arrived in the lobby and warmly greeted her with his sleeves rolled up. "Let me walk you to your office," he said.

She followed his brisk pace down the hall toward his office as he repeated his monologue about the importance of quickly turning sales around.

"I am confident that you can ignite sales. We *must book* new business," he said as they arrived at an office down the hall from his.

She nodded, having expected his marching orders. "I intend to deliver." She was anxious to get started, and nothing would dampen her resolve. Tom was her number-one customer, and that meant the entire sales team needed to adopt an action-oriented customer focus, the hallmark of the Catalyzing Mindset.

He gestured to the folder on her desk. "I'll leave you to review the past sales data and be back in"—he checked his watch—"thirty minutes to introduce you to Debbie Conrad and the others." Placing Debbie at the top of the roster for introductions reflected her status as office manager. She knew Debbie had been with Tom since the beginning, and with an office right outside his, she must know the business inside and out.

•

Debbie appeared to be a hard-working, no-nonsense woman determined to make the trains run on time. Tom had introduced her as his indispensable right hand. While a small smile had emerged on Debbie's face, Kate was sure she had not been swayed by the compliment. Not a yes-person, that one. Probably kept things on an even keel and accepted change only after Tom championed it.

"Here's a package with all of our policies and benefits. You'll need to look over that when you have time, to decide about insurance. Right now, I'll need you to fill out the W4 and I-9, sign the employment contract, and if you wish, complete this direct deposit form." Debbie offered assistance if there were any questions.

Though Kate didn't really need the help, it gave her an opportunity to speak with Tom's gatekeeper. She learned that Debbie's portfolio extended well beyond that of the standard office manager. Debbie handled customer service and finance too—both bearing directly on Sales. She was not officially on the sales team, but she was a key stakeholder. Kate needed her as an ally. Otherwise, she could become an obstacle sitting next door to Tom's office.

"This should do it." Kate handed over the package.

Debbie checked it over. "Looks fine." She reached across her desk to shake Kate's hand and said, "Welcome to the company. Now please join Tom in his office."

•

"Well, glad it is official," Tom said as he stood up. "If you'll follow me, I'd like to introduce you to the staff."

They went to the production floor where employees had gathered. "I'm pleased to introduce you to Kate Hollander, our new vice president of sales. We all thank Kate and Richard for their exemplary service to our country." He continued, making little more than a glancing reference to her prior accomplishments in sales. "Richard served with Kate in Iraq, and he thinks the world of her. I feel certain that his confidence is justified. Let's make her feel welcome."

A short round of applause followed his introduction, and some employees took the time to shake her hand. "Welcome." "Glad to have you." And even a "Good luck." The greetings were friendly enough, and Kate accepted each one with gratitude.

But something about the introduction made Kate squirm —not noticeably, she hoped. Tom's expression of confidence had sounded like more of a wish than a conviction. When the handshakes were over, Richard invited her to lunch at the SoHo restaurant across the street, where he provided more background on the firm's history and current challenges.

"Kate, this is a great opportunity for you—and Davis Printing is lucky to have you. We have good, talented people. I wouldn't have asked you to consider the position if that weren't true. But you need a little background about the sales team you're inheriting."

"Okay, shoot."

"You're replacing Larry McCutcheon. He was a nice guy, and I think at one time he was a go-getter. But he started coasting, and he was far from proactive about getting new business." Richard took a sip of his iced tea. "Between you me, he was nearing retirement, and he pretty much gave up on trying to manage or build the team. Basically, he used his personality and charisma to close his sales. Everybody always said that Larry could charm his way into or out of anything."

"What was the final straw?"

"His numbers were eroding. Steadily. That's one thing. But then he lost a major client."

"Ouch."

"No. It gets worse. He hid the bad news from Tom. Well, you just don't do that. Tom won't stand for being kept in the dark. He fired Larry, and it was definitely the right call. The problem is that, as experienced as Tom is, I don't think anyone had ever flat-out lie to him before. It changed him. He's determined never be out of the loop again. Now don't get me wrong, he was always involved in day-to-day activities, but now he's taken it to the extreme, micromanaging every single thing."

"That's not a smart move."

"Agreed. But we can help him change, with you in Sales. For now, your mission will be to produce results and keep Tom up-to-date. But that may not be as simple as it sounds since the sales team needs a reboot."

2

Getting the Lay of the Land

After lunch, Kate held her first staff meeting. She had prepared by searching online for the company and its products. She did not find a lot, but that told her plenty. Davis Printing lacked the digital footprint and, more specifically, the social-media presence of most of its competitors. This jibed with what Richard had told her. The company relied too much on personal contact and reputation. Davis Printing held a fine reputation but was not aggressively building on it *today.* Inattention to their digital presence could lead to falling sales.

Kate would definitely address building their social marketing, but she wanted to hear her team's priorities first. Without a printing background, she needed to listen to their concerns and expectations before proposing solutions. People—especially those in sales—had uncanny antennas for detecting fabrications and pretense. Gaining insights from them would show respect for their experience. Besides, maybe something was already in the works.

Despite Tom's take-charge directive, listening would establish a team mentality. Immediately pointing out shortcomings would create defensiveness, and the sales team would be less likely to contribute. She wanted to prove she was on their side rather than their adversary. Kate would take time to gather the information she needed and avoid rushing into ill-conceived actions. If that meant a slight delay in progress, she would weather Tom's disapproval.

Regardless, Kate had plenty to offer: willingness to listen and learn, personal integrity, and sales mastery. Dedication to excellence, teamwork, and results. Her primary goal was to build a winning team. She would seamlessly weave together her agenda and theirs to fulfill Tom's expectations.

When she walked into the drab conference room, Tom Davis was standing to her right near a solid-brown Formica-topped conference table surrounded by six chairs that matched neither the table nor each other. Red, blue, tan. Leather, fabric, wheeled, wooden. The beige walls displayed frayed poster-sized copies of flyers, brochures, the Davis Printing logo, and even a business card. Strange that a printing firm would not display fresher products. This room was clearly not a customer-showcase environment. In a high-backed armchair sat a twenty-something-year-old man with thick reddish-brown hair. He wore wire-rimmed glasses on his long, sharp nose and was looking intently at his tablet.

A woman sitting in an armless task chair swiveled toward Kate and gave her a slight nod. Dark skin, light-brown eyes, hair braided in rows straight back from her round face, hanging just below her shoulders. Was she even out of high school?

"Ah, Kate!" Tom was all smiles and turned to the others. "I thought I'd come in and introduce you personally to your sales team. Mitch, Joann, I want you to meet Kate Hollander. I know that her talented leadership will take this team—all of you—to new heights."

Mitch Douglas was *a racehorse waiting to have a derby*

run, according to Richard. He took a quick glance at his screen and lifted his hand for a brief wave before removing a small notebook from his open shirt pocket and jotting a note.

"Hi." Joann Mercer's voice was barely audible. She was the newest and youngest team member, with a three-year tenure. *Underutilized, underconfident, underpaid.*

"A pleasure to meet you both," Kate said.

Tom checked his watch and looked past Kate for a moment, then cleared his throat. "Well, I'm sure you're ready to get this meeting sta—"

In bustled a middle-aged man in khaki slacks and a red short-sleeved polo shirt. He swept his fingers through the tall brown hair atop his head, then patted it back in place. Without so much as a glance at Kate, he approached Tom. "Hey, I just got off the phone with Alice Notley at First Light Stores. I am this close"—the man brought his right thumb and forefinger within a quarter-inch of one another near his right eye—"this close to closing on the catalog job. Four-color, twenty-five thousand units minimum, twice yearly."

And this must be Brian Lewis, Kate thought, the *cocky senior salesman.* Late, and no apology.

The corners of Tom's mouth turned upward, but his raised eyebrows had Kate wondering whether he would wait for a signed contract before counting on the sale. Smart man. "Produce results you never need to lie about." Richard's words were lodged in Kate's mind. Never celebrate without a signature.

Tom turned toward her. "Kate, it's all yours. I know you and the team will accomplish great things." He shook her hand, nodded to the others, and sat down at the head of the table.

Brian sat on a wooden stool near the whiteboard at the far end of the room and crossed his arms. Richard had spoken of him at length. Brian was in his early forties—seeping into middle age, he joked of himself—and had worked at Davis Printing for nine years. Tom told Richard that Brian had expected the VP position and wished Tom had asked him to interview for it. But Brian had not met sales goals recently. He attributed it to the fact that Larry had gotten lazy and stopped producing his share of sales as he neared retirement. Larry—his mentor years earlier—the cause of Brian's poor sales? Not a chance, Kate recognized.

"Thank you," Kate said to Tom, then faced the others. "I'm thrilled to join Davis Printing. I've learned that the most essential principles of leadership are to listen more than talk, to be open to whatever my team brings me—be it a complaint, problem, or idea—and to make my *number one job*"—she held up an index finger—"removing any barriers to the team's success so we can meet, and likely surpass our goals. I will always keep you updated, and I expect that our team will continually share the unvarnished truth. Staying on top of things is critical to our success.

"During my time at MedSurgicals, I led the Sales Department, and we always met, and frequently exceeded, our quotas. After 9/11, I wanted to serve, so I joined the army as a medic, receiving four medals during my three tours in Iraq. There I advanced through the ranks and earned my position as a noncommissioned officer through leadership and by focusing on the mission and my fellow soldiers.

"So, I don't have your printing experience, but I'm excited to learn from you, and *you* have the opportunity to teach me. I'm going to observe, listen, and learn to quickly recommend what we can do to excel. I'll be asking lots of questions since the more I ask, the more I'll learn about our opportunities, customers, and competition. And, I'll expect questions from you. I believe that we'll gain from each other's experience."

Kate paused. Blank faces all around. "I'll start by riding with each of you on sales calls, getting to know our major clients and seeing them from your perspectives. I look forward to learning about the products, as well, so we can rapidly increase sales and satisfaction."

More silence, except for Brian's stool creaking as he leaned back against the wall.

"Okay. Your turn. Questions? Comments?"

Nothing. So, her team had adopted a wait-and-see approach. Their expressions had softened, at least. Mitch was watching her instead of the tablet, Joann was making direct eye contact, and Brian had an intense look on his face.

"Let's start by discussing what you need to succeed. I want *your* ideas on how to boost sales."

Mitch pushed his tablet aside. Maybe a conversation was going to—

Tom's fingertips massaged his left temple, then started rubbing his chin. He squirmed in his chair, his face a frozen mask. The team *might* be ready to talk, but no one could miss the boss's body language. He must not be happy with her listen-observe-and-learn approach. Maybe he saw it as weakness, a reluctance to act quickly and decisively.

The team remained silent. Mitch lightly twirled his pen. Joann opened her mouth but closed it as soon as she glanced at Tom. Kate debated whether to invite Tom to speak or push ahead.

"Can *I* tell you what we need?" Tom finally asked.

"Actually, Tom, it would be best to hear from the sales team first," Kate said before he could continue. "They have on-ground information, recent intel that I'd like to hear before examining the bigger picture."

Tom raised his eyebrows, half-smiled, and clasped his hands in his lap. "Carry on, commander."

Mitch leaned closer to the table. "The problem is

with Production. They miss deadlines all the time, and clients are fed up. If we can't meet our deadlines, we lose our edge. Printing is all about delivery and deadline, deadline and delivery."

Tom leaned forward and faced him, but Debbie came in, waving a message pad, and signaled him out of the room.

After he left, Brian said, "Well, Production is a problem, but if you ask me there's a larger issue: Debbie Conrad." He inclined his head toward the door. "She handles customer service, but she continually sides with irate customers. It's a knee-jerk response with her. She thinks the customer is always right when, in reality, they can be very wrong."

"That's true," Mitch said. "She never asks *us* about the backstory. We make mistakes, sure, but usually, the problem is customers who change orders or delay approving the proofs." He tapped his pen on the table. "And we never hear about the complaint until we're blindsided during the next sales call. They're upset, and we didn't even know there was a problem, what caused it, or how it was resolved, because Debbie kept us in the dark."

Joann spoke up. "I don't have a big problem with Debbie, but I have to say, Tom is constantly applying pressure." She breathed in before continuing softly. "That wouldn't be so bad if he didn't also hover over us and try to micromanage everything. He ignores my suggestions for social-media marketing. He thinks everything can be resolved if we just work harder." She furrowed her brow. "I think we should work smarter, not double down on what we've always done and hope for better results. That's not gonna happen.

"You know, people see me as just an order taker. Well, there are other things I can do to grow sales, even without new funds."

Without acknowledging Joann's issues, Brian complained about Production and brought up pre-press. "That's design and layout," he said pointedly to Kate. "They are slow, slow, slooow."

Kate took a deep breath. "Thanks. These sound like some meaty issues to—"

Vibrations quivered underfoot, followed by a deafening roar. The windows rattled as if pelted by fistfuls of pebbles.

Joann gestured toward the windows. "F-fire! Across the street! Fire!"

The restaurant was engulfed in flames. "Call 911! Do it *now*, Joann!" Kate shouted over her shoulder, already on the move. She ran out the door, heading toward the street.

3

Chaos

Glass splinters, as well as larger lance-shaped pieces, covered the parking lot and street. Flames, orange at their tips and almost white at the base, curved up and out gaping holes fronting the SoHo restaurant. Like a blow torch, the fire shot up with a hiss, radiating intense heat. Kate thought she had left scenes like this behind in Iraq. But now bedlam was alive here, across the street—where she had been sitting just two hours ago.

Pushing aside her shock, Kate scanned the scene. Soot-faced diners stumbled out of the doorway, coughing, rubbing their eyes, looking about as bystanders rushed toward them. The blanket of shattered glass over the street and restaurant parking lot would be a greater danger than the possibility of another explosion. Kate ran into the chaos. She needed to attend to the injured and prevent anyone from carelessly hurting themselves with the glass.

"Yes, yes, explosion, flames!" A well-dressed man on her side of the street was yelling into his cell phone. "Please, they're hurt. We need, we need help. Now!"

Outstanding. EMS would arrive shortly. Time for triage. The people moving on their own power were not her top priority. "Watch the glass!" Kate shouted as one, two, three, four were brought out to the parking lot. Another stumbled outside without assistance.

A young woman knelt beside a gray-haired man lying still on his back across the street. "Dad? Dad!" She screamed waving her hands wildly above her head. "Help us! Anyone!"

Kate scanned the area as she sprinted toward them. To her right, a middle-aged woman in a blackened short-sleeved blouse sat on the asphalt, holding her burned arms up in front of her, bleeding from her right leg. Brian was racing toward the woman, calling, "Tonya!" Kate assured herself that he could handle her injury.

Her eyes shifted to a young man sitting on the pavement, clutching a misshapen arm. His moaning indicated he was breathing, so the elderly man was still her primary concern. She caught a glimpse of Tom staring at the scene, then finished her scan for other victims. On the right, a man lay on his stomach, the back of his shirt burned away, his skin raw. He was moaning but alert. Nearby, a young woman seated on the asphalt had abrasions, her clothes in tatters, but she was talking on her phone.

As she neared the motionless man, Kate called out firmly but calmly. "Tom, can you start herding the crowd to the side? EMS will be here any minute."

Tom hesitated momentarily. "Got it." He walked toward a group of onlookers in the street and opened his arms wide, motioning them back from the street.

Kate reached the elderly man. "Hold steady," she said to the crying woman above him. "I'll do all I can." Tears slid down the woman's cheeks. She took a deep shuddering breath, drawing her lips between her teeth.

Kate knelt beside the man and gently shook his shoulders to rouse him. "Sir! Sir, can you hear me?" Nothing. She gently held two fingers on his wrist—no pulse—bent closer, tilted his head back, and placed her ear near his mouth. No sound, chest not moving. She began chest compressions, her lips ticking off the numbers as she pushed for thirty counts. She raised his chin, pinched his nose with her thumb and forefinger, and delivered two rescue breaths before returning for another thirty compressions. Richard jogged over and stopped beside her. "Can I help?"

"You bet," Kate said just as Brian called out.

"Kate! I need help here. Lots of blood. *Lots* of blood!" Brian's face was ashen, his eyes wide.

"Take over CPR," Kate said to Richard.

"On it."

Absence of breathing was more urgent than anything. *Lots of blood*, a close second. With the man under Richard's care, she raced toward Brian. Blood pulsed from a deep, gaping wound in the woman's thigh. Kate looked into her panicked face. "It's Tonya, isn't it?"

The woman stared at her.

"You're gonna be all right, hear me? You're going to be okay." She brushed away the glass on the pavement and eased Tonya onto her back. Kate pressed her palm over the bleed—likely a damaged femoral artery—and maintained the pressure.

"Got a pen?" she asked Brian.

"A ... *pen*?"

"Pen, yes, pen."

He patted his upper chest with bloody hands, located a pen, and handed it to her.

"Take off your shirt. I need strips of fabric."

This time, he complied immediately and removed his jacket and shirt. He clenched his teeth on the hem of his shirt and pulled. After one sharp, continuous tear, he handed a section to her.

"Okay. Help me with this tourniquet. Raise her leg a few inches." Kate slipped the strip under the woman's leg, wrapped it twice above the wound, and tied it off. She stuck the pen into the loose knot and twisted it until the blood flow stopped.

"Like a faucet," Brian whispered.

"Hold this in place. Stay with her, keep her calm. She's going to be all right. Keep telling her that. But don't let her move."

Wiping her hands on her blouse, Kate returned to Richard. He had stopped CPR. Either the patient had recovered, or CPR had failed. "What's the update?" she asked as she approached. The elderly man's face had gained a light-pink hue.

"I've got a pulse—*and* he's breathing!" Richard's face beamed as if he had won the lottery.

"Hooah!" She pumped her fist in the air. "*Outstanding!*"

Kate leaned down. "You're going to be fine, sir." The man looked up at her. "Richard will stay with you, so you're in good hands. Don't move. Paramedics are on the way."

As the first sirens warbled in the distance, she reassessed the other injuries. *Breathing and bleeding covered for now.* Broken arm, sitting in place. Cell-phone woman still talking. Kate went to the man lying face down in the lot. A burn that large could throw him into shock. "How are you doing, sir?"

"Hurts. It really hurts," he said weakly. But he *did* respond, so he was alert and in touch with his reality—because burns hurt like Hades. He wasn't in shock, but he needed top-notch burn care that only a hospital could provide.

"What's your name?" Kate asked.

"Pete."

The sound of the sirens was getting closer. "Pete, hang in. The medics are on the way. They'll get you to the emergency room ASAP."

The young man holding his arm had started rocking back and forth, moaning. On the battlefield, she would splint the arm, but the paramedics would want to handle that themselves. "I think you broke that arm," she said. "Hold it just like you are. Help is on the way."

She moved to the woman with cuts and scrapes. Still on her phone, a very good sign.

"Hi. What's your name?" Kate asked, interrupting her.

"Hold on, I gotta go," she said into the phone, then pressed the screen and looked at Kate. "Sienna. Sienna Maxwell."

"How are you doing, Sienna?"

"I'm freaking out," she said, staring at her arms as she twisted them slowly.

"I bet you are." Kate looked over Sienna's condition. Severe scrapes, embedded glass, but nothing life-threatening. "Take a deep breath and hang in. You're banged up, but I don't see anything serious. Sit tight. The paramedics will be any second now." As if on cue, two firetrucks and an ambulance turned the corner and stopped in front of SoHo.

Kate ran to the ambulance. "Happy to see *you*. We have five primary patients on the parking lot," she said to the first blue-clad EMT she met. "One's a man, about seventy. He had no pulse, no respiration when I approached him about five minutes ago. We performed CPR, and he's conscious and alert. Over there." She pointed to him. "And we have a woman, looks to be in her forties with burns, lacerations, and a potential femoral bleed. I applied a tourniquet. Hemorrhage is controlled for now. She's with my colleague over there." She nodded toward Brian. "And there's a man with serious burns, another with a broken arm, and a woman with multiple projectile injuries."

The EMT tilted his head to the side. "Lucky for them, you've had some training."

"Um, army medic once." Kate ran a hand down the back of her neck.

"Thanks, miss. We've got it now."

Kate recognized her cue. They were better equipped to lead, anyway. "Okay," she said. "Here if you need me."

As another EMT unit arrived, the firefighters trained their hoses on the burning restaurant, pulling water from the hydrant at the corner of the block. Tom had effectively cleared the street before their arrival.

Kate stepped back, reflecting on how effective triage had been in creating order, setting priorities, and tailoring responses. Paramedics were spreading out among the wounded, continuing care in light of what she had been able to do. One of them took over for Richard with the elderly man, while his daughter chattered away. The man's life had been saved because triage dictated that he be treated first. Tonya hadn't bled out because emergency protocol placed her next in line. The other injured were receiving the care they needed thanks to effective triage. Situational awareness, order, priorities, tailored treatment.

Richard walked over just as one of the EMTs came up to Kate. "You did a great job here," the paramedic said. "I think the old guy will come out okay. Vitals look stable, and he's getting packaged for the hospital now. That pen tourniquet on the lady was creative, by the way." He pointed at Brian, who sat with arms crossed over his bare chest. "You owe someone a shirt."

Kate flashed a grin. "I'm just really glad to see you guys."

"Well, you did a great job delivering emergency care. Driving up on an explosion scene, we expected panic and confusion. Thanks to you, we had a head start." He gave a thumbs-up and walked back to the ambulance.

"Like old times," Richard said. He gave her shoulder a pat.

Tom came over from the sidewalk. Pale-faced, he looked at Kate. "Thank you for what you did here. Un-be-

lievable. I'm glad you were here—I'm glad you *are* here."
He turned to Richard. "Thank *you* for bringing Kate to us."
He took a deep breath and looked around them. "What a
day."

"I certainly didn't do this alone," Kate said. "You
saved valuable time by handling the crowd and confusion,
Richard saved the older man, and Brian"—Kate noticed
Brian standing motionless with his soiled jacket over his
bare shoulders—"he helped his friend handle the severe
bleeding. I must thank Brian." As she left, she said, "We
need to get him a new shirt and jacket. And a pen, for
that matter."

4

Deep Dive

Days after the restaurant explosion, Tom called Kate into his office. "I just got off the phone with the owner of SoHo," he said. "Three of the fire victims have been released from the hospital, and the rest are in good condition."

Kate's heart warmed at the news. She was grateful she had been able to stabilize them until they could get the level of attention they needed.

"The main thrust of the blast went through the big front windows, so the structure remains in good shape. He'll be able to open the business again soon. He wants to recognize you by offering you and a guest dinner on the house. That's the least any of us could do for you."

•

As Kate pored over sales data that afternoon, she half-wondered if *her* business, Davis Printing, could be revived as quickly as the restaurant. Sales figures were not in a *slump*. More like a *trend*. Sales volume was slowing, order size was decreasing, and repeat business had fallen off. The stats revealed a long decline.

Continuing as if nothing were wrong would be foolhardy. Past practices or minor changes wouldn't cut it.

Superficial efforts had already failed. Even seasonal adjustments could not hide the decline. Past promotions, an attempt at a loyalty program, and special pricing had all failed. Sales practices needed a significant overhaul.

She wished she could pull out a magic wand to deliver immediate improvement. But, easy answers could not ignite sales. To actually move the needle, she would need to analyze how to spark both short- and long-term growth. Just as the triage process provided immediate temporary relief before extensive care arrived after the explosion, she needed a two-stage plan for reviving sales at Davis Printing. Acting swiftly to overhaul sales practices and policies that she could immediately sell to Tom. And also developing a longer-term plan, which would probably require investment. Ranking business priorities was just a variation of organizing injuries in the field. Historic numbers would help but would not suffice. Kate needed fresh, creative, practical, and implementable alternatives. To get it right, she had to have firsthand information on the marketplace, customer patterns, product line, and the sales team's practices.

Kate scheduled individual meetings and sales calls with each team member. She had three objectives for these meetings: understanding how each of them performed so she could discover ways to improve effectiveness; understanding what was preventing Sales from crushing its numbers; and building cooperative, trusting relationships among them. She also set a time to meet with Debbie to learn about customer complaints.

She would find remedies that would produce immediate *and sustainable* improvements. No point in moving sales to this quarter that would merely rob future sales. Besides, a mere blip in sales wouldn't help. Entrenched problems required thorough analysis and careful evaluation. Despite Tom's short-term mantra, he needed sustainable improvements to increase the bottom line.

Band-aids wouldn't work. She decided to use what was left of her new job honeymoon period to explore solutions and prioritize actions. Data before diagnosis would ensure stellar results.

•

Kate scheduled Brian first since he was the senior member of the team. And because he felt she had hijacked *his* job. He originally impressed her as a talented, ambitious salesperson yet a master schmoozer accustomed to leveraging his colorful personality. Like Willy Loman, the iconic traveling rep in Arthur Miller's *Death of a Salesman*, Brian probably rode along "on a smile and a shoeshine."[1]

But Kate kept an open mind, and Brian's behavior after the explosion impressed her. He helped his bleeding friend, which demonstrated initiative. He ran toward the scene, not away from it. True, he rushed in response to a friend's call rather than first completing a comprehensive situational assessment, but he could not be faulted for that since he was not a trained medic. Schmoozer though he was, he responded quickly, calmly, and faithfully. He probably saved the woman from bleeding to death and knew when to ask for help. Kate reminded herself that when she asked for the shirt off his back, he gave it to her. She wanted to think the best of him and give him the opportunity to impress her.

"Kate?" Brian poked his head in the doorway.

"Hi, Brian. Come on in." Kate got up, walked around her desk to greet him.

"Good morning," he said cheerfully while looking directly into her eyes. "And how are you this morning?"

"I'm fine, and you?" She motioned toward the chair in front of her desk.

"Kate, I am doing *great*. Do you remember when we first met ...?"

"You made quite an entrance." Kate smiled.

"Well"—he looked down at his shoes—"you got me there. It was the deal with First Light. They need a four-color catalog, and the deal's about to close. We're in the short strokes now."

"That's good news," Kate said. "It has been dragging on a bit, though. Please let me know if there's anything I can do to help you get the signature."

"Oh, don't worry about that. I'm a closer. Always have been."

"So, what's been happening over the past two quarters? I'm not singling you out, but revenues have been going down steadily."

"I agree. We've been in a slump."

"I'm concerned that it's more than a slump. It looks like a sustained trend. What's your analysis?"

"I'm gonna have to push back on that. I've been in this business a long time. Things happen. This is just a temporary *slump*. No one knows why. In any case, First Light's business will ignite sales. Nothing succeeds like success. I promise to make a fresh round of calls all this week. I'll turn on a full-court press. You'll see."

"I'm very eager *to* see the results. How about doing joint sales calls this week?"

"Right. I'm looking forward to it. In the meantime, though, if we can get Debbie Conrad on *our* side so she doesn't believe every customer complaint, that will really pay off."

"I'm talking with her later today. I'll see if we can get more feedback from customers and timely information so we're not blindsided—"

"That's great and all, but she'll probably keep siding with the customers. She can't help it."

"I appreciate your input. Thanks for meeting with me."

"Open or closed?" Brian asked about her office door.

"Open is fine, thanks."

His denial and passive acceptance of current problems were troublesome, but considering the way he handled himself after the explosion, he might be capable of change. Expecting one sale and momentum to right the ship was unrealistically optimistic. He had offered no tangible insights, a concrete plan, or willingness to veer from established practices. His comment about a full court press was promising but if he stayed with tried-and-true-with-just-enough-luck approach, things might now change. His reference to Debbie was finger-pointing rather than accepting responsibility or offering solutions. Well, she would see if things went any better with Mitch.

•

As Kate looked up from her desk a few minutes later, Mitch walked through the doorway. Though he had initially joined the chorus blaming issues on Production and Debbie, Kate hoped that in a private setting, he might be ready to solve problems instead.

"Mitch, good morning. Come on in." She came around her desk and sat next to him in front of her desk.

"Everyone's still talking about how you took charge the other day. That was something!"

"I'm just happy it ended well," she said. "It could've been a lot worse."

"You know your stuff."

"The army trains people very well, and everyone worked together."

"Well, I'm hoping we can work together to get Production moving faster and persuade Debbie to be on our side with customers, at least every once in a while."

"I heard this from Brian, too, and I'll work with Production, naturally. But we have to upgrade our own shop. The problem is in *our* numbers, so we need to own that. Boosting sales is goal one, and it's something within our control."

Mitch grimaced and shifted in his chair.

"You don't agree?"

"Look, I'm sure Sales has room for improvement. We're not perfect. But—and Brian agrees—the real stumbling blocks are in Production and customer service."

"Maybe. I'll be in a better position to judge after I finish my ride alongs. But wouldn't it be great if we could move the needle *in Sales*—and having accomplished that, make our case to the rest of the company to work more effectively with us?"

Mitch ran his hand through his hair. Kate waited for him to start pitching again. "I see your point," he finally said. "I'm not sure how much we can 'move the needle' without cooperation from the other departments, but I'll give it my best."

"That's all I can ask, Mitch. Thank you."

As Mitch left her office, Kate rose to adjust the old-school Venetian blinds on her window. The thickening clouds had darkened the office.

•

Joann Mercer came in next. During the initial staff meeting, Joann was the only member of the sales team who had offered a proposal to move forward. Targeting social media made sense. Davis Printing was currently a digital no-show. Using social media was not only a good idea but a necessary one in the current marketplace.

"Joann, what would Davis Printing gain if you got a green light for a social-media initiative? How would that help you?" Kate framed her question deliberately. Had Joann developed a plan, and did she have specific career expectations?

"*Me?*" Joann hesitated but squared her shoulders. "I'm essentially an order taker here. I'm cold calling on the phone but not online. I also follow up on our customers. And I get a few new orders. Mostly, though, my time is spent trying to maintain major accounts, some of which, quite frankly, are on life support.

"So, what would *I* gain from social media? Growth in a position that is otherwise, to tell you the truth, approaching a dead end. Can we switch to what *Davis Printing* will gain?"

"Certainly. That's what I was hoping for."

Joann leaned forward with a smile. "We as a company would finally jump into the twenty-first century with both feet. If we were the only printer in the region, maybe we could get away without much of a Web presence. But we aren't. Thanks to the Net, customers aren't limited to local or even regional vendors. We can't keep yielding ground to just about every other printer on the planet. I'm not saying we should give up what we have. Brian, Mitch, Tom—especially Tom—have built a lot of personal relationships, which an online presence alone can't touch. I recognize that. I respect that. But it's not enough anymore. Our numbers are telling us this. We have a great story to tell, but if we don't tell it where people are listening, it'll be lost."

"So, what's stopping the shift?"

"Budget—as in no budget, or support. I have the digital skills to take us online. But I don't have a social-media marketing budget, and my time is being misused. I waste too much time offering excuses and hand-holding disappointed clients. We have to deal with the causes instead of the symptoms. We need to increase our ability to produce on time. Our deliveries create negative online comments, and we're not addressing the issue."

"What have you proposed so far?"

Joann's smile faded into a quiet sigh. "Tom listens, but he's not interested. He's made that much clear. His personal touch built the business, and he's convinced that's the only thing that'll expand the business again." She paused. "Should I go on?"

"Certainly, I want your ideas."

"Tom's presence can't grow this business much further. That's not a slam on Tom. He's a great salesman, and that hasn't changed. But *he* hasn't wanted to modify anything else. That's the point. The business, the market, the environment—they've all changed. They adjust to a changing environment. And in printing, digital is no longer optional. It's mandatory."

"I'll be making sales calls with Brian and Mitch to learn how well we work with our customers, or how we don't. Let me get a solid picture of things as they are now. Then you and I will talk further about getting Tom and the others on board with a social-media program and delve into Production issues. I'm not putting you off. I just need some time to find out more."

"I hear you."

"Thank you for your openness. I don't know what will be done, but I promise we'll revisit this conversation. I won't let this go."

•

Kate ate at her desk while she prepared for her meeting with Debbie. Given Brian and Mitch's comments, she had some inkling about Debbie's approach, but she also recognized they used her as their scapegoat. Kate decided she would not challenge Debbie but listen and learn how she approached customer concerns.

Debbie came by Kate's office right on schedule.

"Hi, Debbie. Thanks for meeting with me. You're at the hub of operations here, and I look forward to working with you. And, I want to learn where we're falling short and how issues are resolved. Are there particular patterns to the complaints? What solutions would you suggest? Addressing them will impact current and future sales."

"Well, the complaints almost always center on delivery—missing deadlines. I check the original purchase orders, and it's clear we're behind schedule. It's not a matter of opinion or an in-depth investigation. It's black and white. I have no reason to doubt the customers' complaints. The real problem is why we routinely miss the mark. I think it comes down to unrealistic promises— just to seal a sale. They agree to the customers' timelines without checking with Production on inventory or schedule."

Debbie glanced at the door, confirming she had closed it before continuing. "There's almost no cooperation between Sales and Production. They've got to communicate and coordinate more effectively, or customer complaints will only increase, and we'll all pay the price.

"Richard knows about the issues. Production has improved since he came aboard, and complaints have come down somewhat. But much more needs to be done to keep our customers happy, as well as our production staff.

"We've got to focus on reducing silos so we can work together. We need cooperation, not turf wars. I worry that the constant friction between Sales and Production will trigger turnover in Production, and those skills are difficult to replace."

"I hear you loud and clear, Debbie. Thank you for discussing the issue. I agree. Sales and Production must work together. Let me ask you something else about customer complaints. What is your process for resolving them? What do you do?"

"I listen, and I commit to making things right."

"That's it?"

"That's it. What else is there? The customer is always right."

"That's certainly true most of the time, but do you also consult with Sales and Production?"

"For me, the most important thing is to quickly and decisively respond to the complaint. I don't want to lose a customer."

"I agree that fast action is essential, but shouldn't others be involved? I mean, without input from Sales and Production, some details may be missed. Cooperation might connect some dots, and it would build collaboration."

"Responsiveness is the key. It's up to Sales and Production to get it right the first time. If customers didn't complain, I wouldn't be putting out so many fires. I'm cleaning up after the promises *your* people make." Debbie's face flushed. "Sales needs to get their act together so we can retain our customers."

Kate reminded herself that her goal was to listen, to collect information, and to understand Debbie's perspective. Getting the data she needed was the top priority, not trying to score points by winning an argument. At Debbie's firm stance, Kate moved on to her final question, which Joann had triggered. "What can you tell me about the budgeting process? I've reviewed our budget and would like your thoughts on what's feasible and what isn't."

"Tom is one hundred percent hands-on with the budget. That's the first thing you need to know. He really is the one you should talk to about that. But I *can* tell you this much. Tom cares about the bottom line. He watches it like a hawk, and he's made it *my* job, well, to be *his* hawk. I track budgets and spending closely. He calls it a 'see something, say something' practice to stop problems from escalating. It works for law enforcement, and it's worked for us."

Kate laughed, and even Debbie smiled, then said, "When it comes to the bottom line, we're all a little ... anxious ... lately."

•

Over the next four days, Kate accompanied Brian and then Mitch on their sales calls. She was gratified that both displayed professionalism and perseverance, and they were intent on closing the sale. But, as Debbie reported, they readily agreed to any requests, including overly optimistic delivery dates.

"You need it on the thirtieth? No problem."

"Five days? We can make that happen."

Disregarding realistic timelines was not the only sticking point. On one sales call, Brian undercut the price list. Kate's knew that roughly six out of every ten prospects wanted to discuss pricing on the first sales call. So she was not surprised at how rapidly the subject came up during that call. Brian started off handling the question well. He explained that he had to run the numbers before he could provide a firm quote. When the client appeared disappointed, he vacillated and offered low ballpark pricing. Then the customer balked at the revised number, citing a ceiling figure, and Brian said, "I'm sure we can work something out."

The implied pricing promise emerged without definitive details on the order's scope or level of customization. The result would likely be a low-margin sale or a dissatisfied customer. Using this transactional sales tactic was short-sighted. His primary concern was making *this* sale, without considering how to expand it. He completely failed to explore other opportunities during this valuable face time with his customer. All salespeople wanted to make the sale. However, *great* salespeople aimed higher. They developed loyal, key, profitable customers. On call after call, Brian missed opportunities to understand the customers' organizations and priorities. He never laid a foundation for future sales.

On a joint call with Mitch, he approached the receptionist and asked to see George Pendergast. She replied that he had retired and offered to call Jack Sharp, who now handled most of their catalogs and flyers. Mitch thanked her as his face reddened, and she made the call. Jack met

Mitch and Kate in the lobby, where Mitch immediately launched into a ten-minute pitch along with citing his past relationship with George Pendergast. He implied he knew George well, despite not having known about his retirement. He had lost touch with his customer.

At last, Jack interrupted him. "Good to meet you," he said brusquely, "but we've already contracted for our current requirements. If you have a card, I'll give it to our new purchasing officer."

Mitch extracted his business card and handed it to Jack. "And who is the new purchasing officer?" he asked.

"I'll give him the card, and you'll hear from him when there's a need. Thanks."

They had spent over an hour on a call to a prospective customer without any preparation. Mitch may have thought his old relationship with Pendergast would make this a great call, but he had been out of touch. Mitch wasted time trying to wing it with Jack. And worse, he had not learned about the organization's needs and failed to get the name of the current buyer!

On another call, Mitch was pleased to sell a job designing and printing custom order forms, but he overlooked examining additional opportunities. When a customer cared sufficiently about image to buy branded order forms, additional products would likely help build the brand more. Why not dig deeper and collect more information? Mitch could have upsold the client with additional offerings. He was more anxious to close, get out the door, and move on to the next call than to invest the time to build a relationship for the future.

His priorities were short term. Like Brian, he employed a transactional approach instead of searching for key requirements or developing an effective relationship with the customer. By pitching rather than listening or analyzing, they were unable to present themselves as a trusted source of information or discuss related products and services—things that reliable customers expected and valued.

Kate recognized that both Brian and Mitch smoothly delivered a pitch and exuded charm. But underneath the smooth delivery, the pitch was the same from one customer to the next. Neither of them demonstrated an interest in eliciting or responding to the *customer's* priorities that drove the sales decision. They would be more effective by triggering a broader, more strategic conversation. The best way to serve customers was to listen to their needs, the equivalent of getting all the answers before a test.

What really surprised her, though, was that neither of them talked about Davis Printing as a locally owned business and active member of the community. Any digital firm could sell standard online printing. But only a brick-and-mortar printer offered personal service—customization, proximity, flexibility, and presence in the community.

So, sell the *firm* as well as the services! And not as something extra but a relevant differentiator in the marketplace, one that regularly impacted a customer's decision. Tom must have been unaware that his sales team failed to consistently promote the firm and also failed to think strategically. Nothing was long term.

•

Kate ended her week by tallying insights that went to the very heart of selling. The problems included ineffective communication, reliance on established customers and product lines, embracing a cookie-cutter approach, and failure to get beyond superficial transactional sales. Winging it would not work. Hope was not a strategy. Preparing for sales calls must become mandatory.

These glaring, significant shortcomings meant Kate needed to shift the way Sales operated. It was time to revise their practices and adopt a consultative, engaging approach that would create loyal customers. The printing industry was undergoing change, and they had to adapt to it. Everyone must pay close attention to customers' changing needs, interests, and priorities.

Kate had gained insights into Sales and customer service. Next came Production. She called Richard. "Could you spare a few minutes at nine tomorrow morning? I'll come to you," she said.

5

Analysis

Richard's support for Kate at Davis Printing and his propensity for action, displayed again after the explosion, buttressed her conviction that he would be a proactive partner. The two of them had always spoken openly with one another, so she knew their meeting would be fruitful.

When she opened the heavy steel door to Production, every employee in the pressroom was busy working. She wondered if the shop had looked like this twenty years ago—smudged pale-blue walls surrounding various sizes of printing presses, each probably brought in as the business grew. The workers wore canvas aprons, heavy-duty gloves, sturdy shoes, and safety goggles—a list of safety protocols hung on the right-hand wall. Even with the activity, some looked up as she walked past. Either a visit from someone in Sales was a rare event or they wanted to watch the newest hire. She nodded to them and entered the open door to Richard's office.

"Kate, come on in," he said above the noise of the machines, rising from behind his large oak desk. "Please, close the door. I like to work with it open. It's when the clatter and hum stop that I worry."

"Why am I not surprised?" Kate laughed and shook his hand.

"Coffee?"

"Black, thanks."

Kate sat down in the chair before Richard's desk, put her the manila folder on her lap, and looked around the office while he ran the single-cup coffee maker. The gray cement floor was a continuation from the work floor, but the similarity ended there. His desk and chairs sat on a faded olive-green Berber-carpet remnant. On the spotless light-tan walls hung nothing but a phrase carved into a long polished board behind his desk. And the carved phrase quoted General George S. Patton, of course: "If everyone is thinking alike, then somebody isn't thinking."[1]

A single wooden bookcase stood in the back corner. The top shelf displayed casual photos of his wife. Beside those was a picture of Richard in his desert uniform, leaning against a Jeep with a few enlisted men. SAMPLES labeled the front edge of the middle shelf, which held several acrylic-framed printings and a colorful tri-fold brochure standing on end. The bottom shelf was packed with large manual binders and printing-industry guidebooks. Always by the book.

Richard placed a black mug in front of her on the desk. "Here you are." He took another cup with him to his seat.

"Thank you." She picked up the hot mug and took a sip. "Never kept a taste for cream and sugar after the army."

"Same here." He chuckled as he sat down. "So, what can I help you with?"

"Well," Kate said, "I met with my staff, as well as Debbie, and got some context. Now I need your thoughts. We clearly need changes. So, what do you see as the starting point? You might as well be blunt since there's no need to dance around the issues. There are lots of opportunities for improvement."

"In a nutshell"—he folded his hands around the mug on his neatly arranged desk—"we need to reduce internal friction and get everyone working together. Sales consistently underbids jobs and overpromises on delivery schedules." He paused. "Shall we get into the details now?"

"Absolutely. Shoot." She leaned forward.

"Most late deliveries are *not* due to Production errors or delays. Production is on top of things, but we can't wave a magic wand. Printing takes time. For standard jobs, we need a five- to seven-day turnaround. Your people know this. We can handle occasional rush jobs. But for quite some time, they seem to promise a fast turnaround on *every* sale. We're chronically swamped with rushes. Which puts us in constant crisis, which busts my overtime budget and stresses my employees." He glanced toward the door, then continued.

"To be fair, some delays aren't caused completely by unrealistic promises. Many clients fail to review and accept proofs on schedule. I bet Debbie doesn't hear *that* from the customers. No mystery there. They rarely accept their role in the delays. But Debbie rigidly adheres to her customer's-always-right policy and never gets the full story."

"I see."

"I'll admit, my analysis of the complaints shows we're responsible for about a third of the issues. But delayed proof approvals and unrealistic delivery schedules account for the rest." He took a sip of his coffee, then set it aside.

"Kate, you've always appreciated the unvarnished truth, so here it is: Production views your staff as lounging at their desks, never having to hustle. Production is hard work—we have *hard* deadlines, and we're always on our feet. We hustle constantly. Your people, on the other hand, spend most of their time making calls from the office. When they are in the field, they make unrealistic commitments not only on schedule but also on our inventory. We can't carry everything in our stock. That would waste resources. Your people frequently discount our expertise, requirements, and value to the firm. To them, Production is a minor player in the back of the house."

"Do you think your people have an accurate picture of Sales?"

"Partly accurate, only partly. We need to improve perceptions in *both* units."

"I appreciate your honesty. So, let me dig deeper. What else contributes to the view that Sales has a cushy job? Is it based on performance, is it their demeanor, is it poor commu—"

"Whooa." Richard held up both hands. "This situation has been brewing for a long time. When Larry ran Sales, he blamed Production for late deliveries. We were his blanket excuse for everything. He refused to consider any other aspects. Worse, his opinion spread, so your staff believes we're the culprits holding the company back. And we responded by calling them prima donnas who don't know what it takes to get things out the door. They weren't meeting their quotas, but we were meeting ours. The tension between units kept growing to where it is now. Meanwhile, our growth has been stunted."

"Well, *I* am not Larry."

He grinned. "Not even close."

"So, let's get to work and turn this thing around."

"Don't forget Tom. He's so disappointed with sales, cash flow, and lack of growth so he's micromanaging more and more. He's driving us crazy—and himself— shifting between cheerleading and second-guessing."

"I sensed a rather hands-on approach from him."

"It's damaging productivity and morale. Tom goes directly to *my* staff to check on the progress of an order and reprioritizes work to favor a specific client. You and I know the value of the chain of command. But if someone short-circuits that process and confusion follows. And, that is if you're lucky. If you're not, it's pure chaos muddied by rumor mills and fear. People lie low until they know whose orders to follow."

Kate shook her head. "Does Tom use metrics effectively?"

"He's a savvy guy, don't get me wrong. He respects numbers. But he also listens to gossip, particularly from Brian. They play tennis together. Now, I can't control who Tom plays tennis with, but I give him regular updates on key numbers. And check in with him once in a while to see if he has any concerns. This counteracts some of the gossip and griping he hears, and I hope it'll cut down on his micromanagement. But that said, Brian *and* Debbie have Tom's ear. We need her buy-in to improve collaboration and squash some of the prevailing stereotypes."

"Then we have a clear mission: set our teams straight, garner Debbie's support, and convince our commander we're heading in the right direction."

"Hooah!" He flashed a smile.

"You're smart to keep Tom up-to-date. He needs a steady stream of information. An information vacuum would alarm him and leave him open to rumors."

"Good point."

"And I'll work with you to improve the way our teams interact. There are times when a particular sale requires a rush delivery—but rush orders shouldn't be routine. *We* need to sell what *Production* can deliver, and at a fair price."

Kate placed her folder on the desk. "Now. I saved the best for last. I'll be making a change in Sales that I think you'll find interesting. We'll be collecting customer information so that we can tailor our pitch, something I learned in sales management called Situational Mindsets. At MedSurgicals we used the six Mindsets to pinpoint what was driving each customer and then customized our presentation to meet their interests. We beat our numbers and gained loyal, repeat customers. I think we need this here. Right now, Sales depends on a transactional approach. We pitch and quickly push to close without listening and targeting customer priorities. The transactional approach doesn't serve us. And it won't build our brand as a value-added printing resource. We have to boost our understanding of each customer's current priorities to grow."

Richard pursed his lips. "Situational Mindsets, huh?"

"Mm-hmm. 'Mindsets' are buckets to collect relevant data, detect key issues, and discover the priorities driving an organization's decisions at a point in time. The term sends two messages: First, every *situation*, context, or environment shapes thinking, plans, and goals. They vary as events change because what rises to be top of mind shifts. And second, the Mindsets are *dynamic.* Addressing old priorities wastes time and resources since we're not closing. Think about the explosion. The owners currently face different issues today than before it happened."

"Anyone would after a disaster like that," Richard said.

"True, but in every organization, conditions can shift rapidly. Few things are stable for long. You had firsthand experience with that in the army. You weren't fighting the same way the army did in Korea or Vietnam. You had to adjust to dynamic conditions and changing enemy tactics or fail. "

"Darned straight."

"Adjustments are just as important in business. Practices change. Resources get reallocated. I may not know the printing industry well, but I know it's different than it was just a few years ago. If we don't understand what's driving our customers' thinking and requirements, we aren't likely to make the sale. "

"How'd you use Mindsets to sell medical equipment?"

"One of our customers valued industry-leading products but later preferred to purchase the most reliable equipment. Knowing that we moved from spotlighting award-winning products to concentrating on quality, reliability, and guarantees. Customer visits with physicians were short, so we had to hone in on what was currently driving them."

"Smart and effective. You must've had really talented salespeople."

"No more talented than our team is. At MedSurgicals, we had to drop the fantasy that we always knew what the customer wanted. False assumptions get exposed by reality."

Richard furrowed his brow. "What do you mean?"

"Our company suffered a big hit. We lost a client—and by 'client,' I mean a whale, a major chain of clinics. Losing that was painful, but it opened our eyes. The customer was focusing on international capacity, not industry-leading products. Why had we missed that? The client never mentioned it, but truthfully, none of us thought to ask." Kate shrugged her shoulders. "So, we blew it. But we learned from our mistake and started using Situational Mindsets. When we drafted new pitches targeting each Mindset, it all clicked. We realized nothing was ever a final priority. Customers constantly moved their goalposts."

"How did you keep up?"

"Easy. We developed questions to uncover which Mindset currently drove the customer's thinking. We needed to understand their current circumstances from *their* point of view. Rejecting the one-size-fits-all strategy enabled us to match our presentations to their Mindsets. It was an adjustment, but it made the job more interesting—and the numbers, the numbers told the tale. Our closing ratio skyrocketed. Sales went through the roof, and we developed loyal customers, to the point that they called *us* when they needed something. It also generated lots of referrals. We transformed ourselves from being just a vendor to a valued partner. It sure beats guessing what the customer wants."

Richard chuckled. "Sounds like a mind-reading act."

"Nothing clairvoyant about it. Asking questions and listening work, and I expect to mirror those results here. The key is focusing on the *customer's* needs, the *customer's* goals. Which aligns with Debbie's customer-is-always-right principle."

"That should make her happy."

"We'll all be happy when it pays off. It feels like a major change at first, so I expect some resistance from the sales force. That's normal. But closing sales turns doubters"—she snapped her fingers—"into converts."

"Catchy slogan. You've certainly got *my* attention."

"I'm glad because Situational Mindsets can help us build cooperation between our departments too." She reached into the folder she had brought with her and handed him a sheet of paper. "Here's an explanation of the Situational Mindsets. I'll be handing this out to my team, but using these elsewhere within Davis Printing would improve the communication between departments too. It values diverse viewpoints which can build rapport. Concentrating on what's important will create a common mission where our units can work together. I'm convinced that the Situational Mindsets framework will deliver results and build a productive alliance between our units."

"I can see how it increases sales volume, but how will it improve unit collaboration?"

"Mindsets expands our thinking and appreciates a range of perspectives. You learn that each point of view stems from objective factors and adds value. It squelches subjective personal opinions or agendas and replaces it with objective analysis. By considering all Mindsets, we can jointly discover what's best for the company *at this time*. Everyone offers their two cents, which is necessary, given the complexity facing us today. No one has all the information needed to make the best decision. We have no choice but to listen to each other, consider what we know, identify alternatives, and then evaluate the best path forward. Respect for Mindsets fosters personal respect and engagement. It may not happen overnight, but it will happen."

"Well, how would you specifically use Situational Mindsets to address the tension between Production and Sales?"

"Right now, Sales predominantly uses a Catalyzing Mindset targeting making a sale, beating the competition, and growing the customer base. This means focusing on retaining customer accounts and providing solid customer service. And there's nothing wrong with that. Sales are critical to our success.

"But success also depends on getting the product out the door. And to do that, the focus has to be on efficient internal operations. This reflects the Performing Mindset, which prioritizes standardizing operations, improving workflow, reducing costs, and improving quality."

Richard ran a finger down the list. "I see it."

"Right now, Production operates from a Performing Mindset. However, these Mindsets can clash if taken out of context. Sales prizes market realities and agility, while Production seeks to deliver quality, excellence, and efficiency. Neither is wrong. We need both, so we have to discover ways to connect those viewpoints. After all, our goal shouldn't be one unit's success but organization-wide success."

"Amen to that."

"These Mindsets emphasize different data sources. Sales naturally focuses on *external* market input and events. In contrast to Production's concentration on *internal* information and statistics. Without valuing both, Sales would likely continue to accept rush orders despite its impact on Production, and Production would still label the sales staff as not pulling their weight. You can see how a blaming culture emerged.

"You said Production thinks Sales has it soft. The flip side is that Sales believes Production has it easier. They work as a team, don't have to travel, and have unit goals, whereas salespeople are often on the road by themselves and are always under pressure to make their numbers. We see the flaws in both, and we also recognize that both perform difficult and vital services critical to our success. There's no way to determine who contributes more. Does Sales contribute forty percent to success and Production sixty? It can't be measured and it probably changes. So each unit must contribute one hundred percent"—she paused—"all of the time."

"How do you propose we smash these impressions?" Richard asked.

"We bridge different views with information, new solutions, and—this is crucial—with respect for how each unit contributes to overall success. The good news is that bridging mindsets cancels the impression that one is less important or a stumbling block. Honestly, it can be difficult to extinguish stereotypes. The smart move is to shift the discussion from assumptions and feelings to facts and outcomes. By exchanging information, we can promote understanding and alignment.

"Working together, we can kick-start the process. Right now, we know there are too many rush orders. Sales can establish new procedures for rush jobs to take the pressure off of Production. And we can specify a proof-turnaround time in our contracts so the customers own their role in meeting the schedule. These doable steps will signal our commitment to joint problem-solving. Hopefully, Production will see and appreciate those efforts, and our people can work out valid rush orders together. Improving coordination like this serves both units. As we achieve results, I believe we'll see improvement fairly quickly."

Richard chimed in. "And you and I could show our commitment to working together by attending each other's staff meetings on occasion. That would improve communication and preempt problems. We'll discover new options while reshaping opinions and respect."

"Great idea," Kate said. "Sales is meeting next Tuesday at nine thirty if you'd like to join us."

"Love to. Production meets the next day at eight thirty?"

"Wouldn't miss it," Kate said, adding the appointment in her phone's calendar app.

Someone knocked on the door—loudly.

"Come in!" Richard shouted.

One of the Production employees entered, wiping his hands on a towel.

"Gee, Ron, you don't have to break the door down."

"Sorry, Richard. It's never closed, and the machines are so loud ..." He pointed back over his shoulder.

"What can I do for you?" Richard asked.

The man pulled a piece of yellow paper from his pocket. "We need seven hours of overtime."

"Tell me more?"

"Three rush orders're stacked up."

"What a surprise." Richard glanced at Kate, one corner of his mouth lifting a fraction. He looked back at the man and asked, "Can we do it? Is the staff on board?"

"Yes. Just for today, though."

"You got it. I'll authorize it now. Come on in and say hi to Kate, our new VP of sales."

After Ron left, Richard looked at Kate. "I rest my case."

"I can see that, so let me ask you—just for practice—what are your current Situational Mindset priorities?"

He perused the Mindsets list, then sat forward. "My goal is to improve productivity *and* build toward a profitable future."

"Anything else?"

"Well … I care about cost and quality, but my greater concern is building our production capacity. We need newer technology and more staff for a prosperous future."

"Okay, Richard. Translating those goals, you're functioning with two Mindsets. You operate from a Performing *and* a Challenging Mindset."

"Can you do that? Operate from two different Mindsets?"

"Sure. While most people use one at a time, some use two or three. It can work, but trade-offs have to be made. The old mandate to work faster, cheaper, and better earns the typical response: which do you want first? But you've already sequenced your Mindsets. From what I heard, you currently place greater emphasis on the Performing Mindset with a focus on quality and production. But you know when that's ironed out, you're also thinking on more-strategically. For example, recruiting me reflects a strategic perspective that positions the firm for the future."

"Right you are. Productivity takes precedence at the moment. But as soon as we have that under control, we've *got* to examine the bigger picture to ensure our future. Unless something explodes, and a fire has to be put out."

Kate's laughter filled the room.

"What's so funny?"

"Besides your cheesy humor, I just realized how much we're in sync—focusing on immediate issues before we pivot to large-scale issues that are coming. The difference is that I'm likely to move from the Catalyzing Mindset to the Developing Mindset, to establish new systems, policies, and accountabilities. But we'll both be working to build for the future."

"This Mindset thing is fascinating. Which one do you think drives Tom?"

"Good question. Since Tom concentrates on both

sales and financial position, I believe he currently—and I stress currently—operates from two Mindsets. His focus on sales reflects a Catalyzing Mindset, while his concerns about cost containment and the bottom line are priorities of the Performing Mindset. Which do you think takes precedence?"

Richard quickly responded. "Sales."

"I agree. Maybe that's because I'm new, and he knows you're doing a great job. But here's a caution: having two Mindsets can create confusion and uncertainty. When you can't predict what's driving the boss, you keep your head down and get reactive instead of proactive. The last thing we need is an ostrich mentality."

"So, is a dual Mindset a fatal leadership flaw?"

"No, not at all. If Tom understands his Mindsets and communicates them effectively, everyone can get on board. This can build confidence that aspects are covered, and our future is bright. So, let's start working with Situational Mindsets and encourage Tom to reassess his goals and communicate them so everyone will buy-in. This process might also reduce his urge to meddle."

"That would be wonderful," Richard said. "It should put his mind at ease, increase his confidence in us. Maybe cut down on his hovering."

"Well, I know I need to keep him in the loop. What's your schedule for updating Tom?"

"I report in on Tuesday and Friday—with the explicit understanding that any deviations or surprises will be shared immediately. You could suggest that schedule if it works for you."

"Right now, I have to build Tom's confidence in me, so I'll keep showing up at his door until he tells me not to. Hopefully, over time, it can be less frequent. Talking about sharing, shouldn't we commit to sharing updates with our staffs? We need to keep everyone current."

"Let's make updates a weekly agenda item in our staff

meetings and see if we can turn things around," Richard said. "I expect the change will impress Tom." He leaned back in his chair and stretched his arms above his head. "We've got a good start, Kate." His eyebrows went up. "You know, even though *our* plans are solid, and we'll influence Tom, keep in mind that others do too."

"As you said, there's Brian ..."

"... and Debbie. We need to get her commitment also."

6

Influencing

Energized after meeting with Richard, Kate was tempted to go directly into Tom's office and announce her plans to boost sales, increase market penetration, and improve coordination. She resisted the impulse and went to her own office to think. She realized that plans between the two units would shortly have to be expanded to encompass the entire organization. She gazed out the window.

Across the street, a crew had gathered outside SoHo. Ace Contracting, according to the signs on the work trucks. A stocky, bald man dressed in jeans and a plaid shirt pointed from clipboard to restaurant as he spoke to the workers. Two other men and a woman nodded occasionally, glancing toward the storefront. After tucking the clipboard under one arm, the man received a high five from each of the workers, and everyone entered the restaurant with a smile. A cohesive, *collaborative* team.

Collaboration involved more than cooperating and exchanging information with Richard's team. Sales needed to act as a team among themselves and across the organization. And they needed to work in tandem with customer service. In fact, everyone had to commit to being on the Davis team, or joint efforts would eventually fail. Mere compliance would not work. Everyone had to be fully committed. That meant Debbie's backing was essential, not only on customer service but to win Tom over to creating a different culture. Debbie was Tom's top influencer and would gatekeeper. Kate would ensure they became allies rather than adversaries.

Customer service could not remain only Debbie's domain. Its role had to be integrated across the firm. As Sales turned from a transactional approach to consultative sales, customer service would take on a new dimension in providing feedback. There should be little daylight between Sales, customer service, and Production. Would Debbie go along? ... Would *Tom* go along?

That was the real question. Kate's initial impression was that Tom would resist change he did not initiate. His trusted Debbie, but Larry and low sales had diminished his trust in Sales. Although Kate would work on restoring Tom's faith, her first step would be getting Debbie in favor of a proposal for greater collaboration. It was the best move. But before Kate could build an alliance with her, she needed to propose an initiative Debbie could support.

Kate planned to meet with Debbie to build their relationship and address her staff's concerns. Both Brian and Mitch felt shackled by Debbie's siding with customers. Kate would show them that she followed through on this sore point and smoothed the way for better customer service. As for the approach ... she opened a new document and recalled Debbie's goals and concerns.

Debbie's current hot buttons were customer service, teamwork, staff retention, and morale. Kate recorded Catalyzing and Protecting Mindsets at the top of the page. Under this heading, she listed her strategy for the meeting with Debbie:

- Focus on customer satisfaction

- Highlight ways to build morale

- Boost high-performing culture

- Retain talent and customer service

- Respect her position and experience

Knowing that the Protecting Mindset preferred to approach change cautiously, she added:

- Propose a gradual shift from existing practices but keep Debbie informed and in charge

She called Debbie's office. "Hey, it's Kate. Do you have twenty minutes to meet with me today?"

"No time like the present," Debbie said.

"Great. Be right there."

•

Entering Debbie's office, Kate noticed again her penchant for organization. Her desk was not bare, but folders were perfectly aligned in a stack on one side and tiered metal boxes on the other. Quite a contrast to the maze of documents obscuring the top of Tom's desk. He might know where everything was, but she doubted it. It probably held not only his work but details on everybody else's. Tom's disorganization increased his reliance on Debbie. She was a talented, organized professional who could become a great asset. Kate was eager to work with Debbie.

"Thanks so much for seeing me on short notice," Kate said. "Although I'm new, I know we share a common commitment to customer satisfaction. I see opportunities for Sales, Production, and customer service to better serve our customers. I've talked with Richard, and we're going to iron out glitches and improve relationships between our units. For example, Sales will curtail making promises that Production can't keep. We're instituting a process to reduce missed shipping deadlines too. Our updated policies should lessen unwanted overtime, which has been impacting morale. We're both committed to preventing problems before they arise."

"You don't know how delighted I am to hear that, Kate."

"Now, there may be additional opportunities to boost efficiencies and coordination. Richard and I want to improve our track record with our customers. One way is learning from you about trends and patterns you observe, which should reduce future complaints while retaining the response time to customer issues. I'd like to discuss a pilot joint customer–complaint process with you. Specifically, I would like to ask you to lead a group to study and analyze complaints. My thought was that it would include customer service *and* Production *and* Sales. All of us working together. The pilot would be only three months so we can evaluate its effectiveness and revamp based on the group's proposals. I haven't run this by Tom yet since I wanted your input first. The team would include you, Joann from Sales, and Ron from Production. With the team researching complaint causes, we should be able to improve service, retain customers, and build our brand."

Kate paused and waited for her response.

Debbie raised her eyebrows. "Richard is okay with this?"

"Absolutely. He wants to improve collaboration and find creative solutions as much as I do. We can move forward in many ways. To start, we'll attend each other's staff meetings to improve effective communication and build relationships. We'll also mandate that Sales require a five- to seven-day turnaround, giving Production the time it needs to meet the schedule."

"Tom would need to approve this." Debbie's voice had lowered a half octave.

"I wanted to hear what you think before speaking to him. I see benefits, but I wanted to check with you to be sure this is the right path. From what I've seen, everyone would benefit, but there may be things I've missed.

Your experience is critical here. Would you support a short-term joint customer-complaint arrangement that will enable us to grapple with the issues and find ways to improve our service?" Kate was telling the truth, but she purposely tuned in on Debbie's Protecting Mindset to minimize the extent of the proposed change.

She continued. "From what I've seen, if you work with Sales and Production we can identify ways to turn the situation around."

Debbie looked thoughtful. The silence was a bit uncomfortable, but Kate waited it out. Finally, Debbie said, "I see potential benefits to a pilot program. It would increase our abilities with customers and within the firm. It's worth a try. And I like the opportunity for all of us to work together. The pilot has limited risk and expense. We should give it a try."

"And Tom should be pleased since it will likely improve the top and bottom line. So, you're in?"

"Yes. The pilot could add value. We all should be working together. I know some folks in Sales view me as a problem, but we really want the same thing—a successful business. Count me in."

"Wonderful. I also want to share with you that I'll be proposing different CRM software. An up-to-date system could track complaints and help detect patterns so we can address issues quickly. It would also enable Sales to stay in close touch with our current clients and help us identify more. And it could help you monitor our resolution processes."

"We already have a system to keep track of customers." Debbie placed a hand on her desktop computer.

"Yes, but the existing program doesn't provide the analytics of the newer software. And we need a system where we can capture more customer information to help our sales team target customers more effectively, track the sales history, and proactively communicate with clients to stay top of mind."

Debbie's hand slid to her lap, and she shrugged. "It's true that what we have doesn't do all that. But fancy products come with fancy high prices, I'm sure."

Kate shook her head. "Not as much as I expected, especially compared with the sales we lose spending time on administrative tasks that this system could do for us. And we have the option of a monthly trial subscription to make ensure that it pays dividends before we commit. Do you think it's worth a try?"

"I certainly don't object to better efficiency, as long as it delivers, and we can afford it."

Kate stood. "Great. I'll discuss it with Tom shortly and circle back to you on next steps."

•

Kate sat spinning a paper clip atop her desk. Tom's acceptance was essential. Her approach must spotlight his current Performing and Catalyzing Mindsets. She would start by discussing the need to accelerate sales, reduce customer complaints, improve coordination between units, and increase ROI. Mentioning that Richard's and Debbie's support for the changes promised seamless implementation, especially as she mentioned the CRM system. She would close with the Situational Mindsets consultative sales approach. It was a solid approach.

However, increased costs needed careful attention. To gain Tom's support, additional expenses had to be limited in amount and duration until revenue growth justified the cost. The CRM package would not be a heavy budgetary hit, and the pilot customer-service team would not cost anything but employee time. With Debbie as part of that team, customer feedback could be assessed swiftly and accurately and improvements implemented seamlessly. All tracked with a CRM system that could generate reports for Tom. The only other expenses would be connected to Joann's online efforts, but Kate expected measurable results to outweigh the eventual cost.

Now, how to ensure a successful meeting arrangement— an informal knock on his door or a dedicated meeting? Tom probably harbored some concerns since she had not made moved as swiftly as he had hoped. A knock on the door would imply a spur-of-the-moment conversation rather than an in-depth presentation or proposed initiative. Since Tom was a face-to-face guy, she called to set up a morning meeting before he got distracted by events.

"Kate," he said in reply. "I was hoping we could have a sit-down. Why don't you drop by now? I have fifteen minutes free."

"If possible, can we set aside at least thirty minutes? I've been strategizing with Richard and Debbie, and we've developed some ideas I want to share with you. Would tomorrow morning work?"

He was silent for a moment. "Eight in the morning. Not too early for you?"

"It's perfect." At eight, fewer distractions would come up, and arriving an hour earlier than usual indicated his sense of urgency.

•

Kate had set her alarm earlier instead of missing her run short to arrive before the meeting. She pushed herself up the foothill paths harder than usual, her adrenaline flowing. She showered quickly and ate a healthy breakfast and headed out to what she hoped would be a turning point for Davis Printing.

At 7:45, she arrived at work pumped and optimistic. When she walked in, Tom's door was ajar. Going into his office now was an option, but this was *her* meeting. She should keep it as scheduled, not a moment sooner or later.

At 7:59:30, Kate gathered her documents and walked down the hall. His door was still open. "Good morning, Tom," she said as she entered. With an open hand, he motioned her to take a chair in front of his desk. He remained seated behind his desk.

A conventional approach to this meeting would have been to open by recounting her meetings with Richard and Debbie. Instead, Kate elected to open with a broader timeline since it wouldn't let him sidetrack the discussion into his ready-made conclusions.

"Tom," she said, "we have the talent to up our game in Sales. But we have to adopt a different approach. We need to go after bigger clients, we need to shift to a consultative approach, and we need to decrease complaints."

Tom's eyes widened a bit. "Well. And I thought you were just here to report on sales activity. Good to hear this large scope."

Having secured his attention, Kate jumped in all the way. "My staff and I are going to build working partnerships with our customers so that we become their go-to printer, the only call they make when they need printing services."

"I like the sound of that. I've always been a relationship guy." Tom sat forward.

"Exactly. Customer relationships are one of the key advantages we have over online players. That's why we have to take more advantage of those connections in each of our sales calls. But we have other opportunities we should leverage too. We can build our brand using social media."

"Hmm. It sounds like we just entered expensive territory." His hand rubbed his chin.

"Not really. We are going to take it slow and document impact before we jump into anything. Joann has the skills and interest in developing our online presence. I've had some productive meetings with her. She's anxious to pursue digital sales. We haven't been using her expertise as fully as we should."

"What's that going to do to building *relationships*?"

"Only good things, Tom. First, Joann's duties can switch from a follow-up role to proactive sales. She's proven her skills with booking phone sales and handling customers. We can modify her job to stay connected with our customers and reach out to new ones." Kate gave him a moment to digest that. "Besides, the change will give Brian and Mitch more-frequent contact with their customers since they will be doing their own follow-ups. And clients won't feel they've been handed off to some-one they don't know right after they place their order."

"More contact is a plus, yes." The chin rubbing stopped.

It was a welcomed sign of progress. "There's more. Joann can concentrate on bringing in B2B customers, and not just locally. Digital is absolutely key for that custom-er pool."

"Larry did let B2B slip."

"We're going to need some marketing support to build our brand and attract B2B business ..."

"That's where I have to put the brakes on, at least for now. I *will* commit to funding limited marketing support, but only *after* we have proof of a return and after we get our books healthy again."

"Sounds reasonable enough." Kate had expected his reluctance, but planting the idea had produced more than she thought it would. A small but a significant victory. He had started to think about funding digital marketing. It was time to mention plans that assured rewards with-out a financial investment.

"Now I'd like to address customer issues. By far, most complaints center on missed delivery deadlines. But the vast majority of those aren't production problems. Cus-tomers create most of them. We must help them realize their responsibility in staying on schedule. Moving customers to that point calls for greater collaboration between Sales and Production. I admit Sales has been made it difficult for Production to meet schedules. Richard and I are fixing this with new protocols and a new order form where the customers commit to a specific number of days for approving proofs. We'll start using that immediately."

Tom relaxed back on his chair.

"Even better, Richard, Debbie, and I devised a coordinated customer-service plan to help turn things around. It'll be on a trial basis until we evaluate its effectiveness, but we expect this to reduce complaints, improve returns, and build our reputation. Debbie will lead a cross-functional team that also has a representative from Sales and one from Production. The three of them will evaluate and resolve customer complaints. A united effort will uncover issues and identify practical solutions that enhance our brand. Happy customers are repeat customers, who also make referrals. An immediate effect will be fewer complaints and therefore, a reduction in the costs of resolving them. But these are just the first steps."

Tom hastily said, "Debbie's okay ...?"

"She's for it, and Richard too. We all agree we must aggressively iron out gaps and inefficiencies to not only serve our customers and improve ROI. One step is reducing overtime. Another is to use a different CRM package to organize our contacts and collect relevant customer data."

"We have a system."

"Yes, but it's a dinosaur compared with what's available now. Every day we use it, we miss opportunities to stay in touch with our customers. We need a higher profile, and we need to reduce admin time. A good CRM system will support a more proactive approach to sales and keep us top of mind with our customers."

"Kate, you know as well as I do sales are down. This

isn't a time to invest in state-of-the-art software."

"Of course." She was prepared for his Performing Mindset cost concerns. "I agree with you. The software I'm proposing is cloud-based and offers a monthly subscription. We can try it out for a few months and see if it's worth it. The investment is minimal. It has a proven track record, and uploading our existing database to this service will be seamless. Down the road, I'm not sure that will be possible because our current system may be too old to interact with future CRMs." She handed him a cost proposal.

"Well, I'm glad you evaluated this so thoroughly." He scanned the fee schedule. "Okay. Let's test drive it for a quarter. Provide a before-and-after analysis to gauge its impact."

"Excellent." She smiled. "Thank you. The package will give us a deeper understanding of our customers. This will improve pricing, track orders, and scheduling. We can segment our customers by profit margins too. And this CRM will provide you with timely information. You'll have it all at your fingertips to monitor progress." This had to be music to his micromanager's ears, and she continued singing the same tune.

"With the increased sales I anticipate, we'll need this system. It'll reduce administrative time so our field sales team can devote more time to selling. I'm confident that within ninety days, the software will show significant benefits. Then we'll evaluate thoroughly and determine what steps will be best for us."

"Okay. ROI *sounds* promising, any other plans?"

"Yes. Sales has focused far too much on making single transactional sales. Don't get me wrong. I want to capture any potential sale. A bird in the hand is a bird in the hand. But we can't limit our vision to single transactions. We need a consultative approach where we listen to the customers' needs, build their trust in our services, and foster strong connections that make us their one-stop-shop printer.

"The Sales Department will be using Situational Mindsets, a method to identify and target current customer needs. We can adjust rapidly to changing requirements and promote our other services. After all, we offer much more than many other printers, and we must position Davis Printing as each customer's primary and complete printing source. We'll build customer loyalty and gain referrals as a result."

Tom smiled his toothy smile. "That's a practical, wide-ranging approach. I like it. But what does this mean for your staff? Are *they* on board?"

"I wanted to run it by you first. With your go-ahead, I'll outline it to them and help them make it work. They're talented and should adjust to it with coaching. As for customers, they'll welcome it. They want to feel in control, and this change highlights their goals."

"How long before we see results?"

"Salespeople are irresistibly attracted to closing *the* sale. It's a hard-wired trait. So, I expect this shift will take a few weeks. But as soon as they see results, they'll become advocates. Nothing excites a salesperson more than success. Consultative sales can turn occasional customers into steady customers. *They* are the richest source of business over the long haul. And growing sales from existing customers is more cost-effective than fishing for new ones."

"Amen to that." Tom grinned again. "Let's get started."

"Can I ask one more thing of you before we close this out?"

He furrowed his brow and looked at her over the top of his glasses.

"I appreciate the green light, but would you consider kicking off these plans? It would be great if you championed the cross-unit collaboration and customer focus at an all-hands meeting."

He smiled. "Happy to support these initiatives. It's great to hear things are coming together. I'll schedule the meeting as soon as possible."

Tom got up and came around to the front of his desk, extending his hand to Kate. Their handshake was a warm one. He clearly welcomed becoming the champion for these organizational changes and seeing both her initiative and her work across the organization.

Hooah, she thought, heading back to her office. She had Tom's buy-in. Now the trick would be winning the same support from her staff.

7

Situational Mindsets

Although Tom pressured Kate to immediately and decisively reboot Sales, she wisely elected to study her terrain before developing her strategy. Like a military leader, she would act only after effective analysis and planning. No need to venture out with inadequate supplies, storm the wrong hill, or start an offensive under adverse conditions. She wanted to avoid provoking failure by implying that they lacked skills, that she alone would transform Sales, or that their jobs were on the line. Introducing change without alienating those responsible for implementation required a delicate balance between truth and tact.

Her team had most of the skills required for strong sales, but they needed to adopt new practices. Her primary goal for the next staff meeting was to introduce Situational Mindsets. With her support, they would discover that the Situational Mindsets consultative approach was simple and rewarding. It would pay off for everyone.

She would kick off the meeting by outlining the actions she had already taken to address their concerns. That would position her as their champion. A leader who would advocate and deliver for them. A part of the team. These were things she aspired to anyway, but boosting her credibility was essential to winning their support for Situational Mindsets.

Kate placed a fresh erasable black marker on the tray of the whiteboard. Almost time to start. Today's meeting would reposition the Sales Department.

Joann arrived first, and Brian and Mitch followed shortly after.

"I'm telling you, he's *not* gonna make it to the pros. He's too—" Brian's mouth closed as he looked at Kate and then the clock on the wall.

Just in time, Kate thought as they took the two empty chairs in front of her desk.

Joann had opened her iPad and set it in front of her at the corner of Kate's desk. Mitch and Brian were empty-handed.

"Hey, Joann, take some notes for me," Brian said as he turned to face her.

"We can compare our notes later if you wish," she said without raising her head.

Building a cohesive team would require some time, Kate thought. Might as well start now. "We're going to cover a lot of ground today. First of all, I spoke with Tom last week, and I want to update you. He agreed to a three-month trial for better CRM software. He'll be announcing that at the company-wide meeting later this week. It's a decade ahead of what we've been using, and it's an exciting opportunity for us.

"Getting loyal, repeat business requires tracking customers, identifying their purchasing patterns, and then sending them messages with special offers tailored to their needs. With this CRM, we can document existing customer relationships, and it will enable you to have more data at your fingertips. Having up-to-date research will build our book at the same time."

Mitch grinned. "I like *that*."

"While we're at it, let's not give up on former customers, those who have drifted away from us. With less paperwork, we'll have more time to connect, more time to reestablish those relationships.

"Best of all, the software will provide a common platform with customer service, enabling Sales to view and respond rapidly and effectively to customer inquiries and concerns. There will be a short learning curve. I found it remarkably intuitive and user-friendly after a one-hour tutorial. You're going to do great things with it and spend less time on admin."

Their responses varied from cautious nods from the guys to a broad grin from Joann. This was not the eager response Kate had wanted. Time to move on.

"We've all discussed the delivery problems. Customers judge us on the performance of the entire organization, regardless of where a problem initiates. We blame Production, Production blames us, and customer service remains in the dark about what actually happened. Richard and I agree that we must develop a new approach to minimize late deliveries. He's committed his unit to meet any seven-day turnaround for standard orders."

Brian sighed.

"And we're developing an order form that includes a customer commitment to a specified turnaround period for approving proofs. It's time we educate customers about their role in keeping things on schedule. That will go a long way to ensuring on-time delivery ."

Heads nodded in agreement.

Riding this modest bump in momentum, Kate said, "Production will regularly ensure a seven-day delivery. However, we need to coordinate with them for rush orders so they can gauge their workload and inventory. They'll do everything they can to accommodate valid rush projects. However, Production needs to work within a schedule and reduce overtime costs."

The nodding stopped, and Brian crossed his arms.

"Not every order requires a rush. And a small rush job can shove some big order out of the queue." Kate shifted to the big picture. "That hurts the firm's bottom line, *our* firm's bottom line. We've got to make a profit if we want to stay in business.

"Pricing must reflect the cost of rush projects. I'm not asking you to spitball it here. We'll update our estimate software to incorporate the cost of expedited orders. This is in line with our practice of charging for premium paper, embossed orders, saddle stitching. If a customer wants a fast turnaround, they should bear the cost."

"I hate to nickel and dime a customer," Mitch said, "let alone a new customer."

"We're talking about a lot more than nickels and dimes. Missed deadlines create a majority of customer complaints. Adding a fee will help us meet both schedule and budget. It's a win–win. This will reduce complaints, overtime, and aggravation on *everyone's* part," Kate reiterated. "Only customers who really need expedited delivery will be asked to pay for it. The up charge will be minimal, but it'll have a significant impact on our numbers. It might even put a smile on Tom's face."

Brian chuckled quietly.

"Let's move on. You've mentioned issues with Debbie's customer service. I presented a proposal to her, Richard, and Tom, and they agree it's worth a try. We're forming a three–month customer–service team, including Debbie and one member each from Sales and Production. Tom will be announcing this, as well. Richard assigned Ron from his department. Joann, you'll represent Sales as that group examines ways to handle persistent issues and effectively resolve uncommon ones."

Joann's typing stopped, and she looked up, her face beaming.

"Through you, we'll gain perspective from the other departments and have direct input."

"About time," Brian whispered to Mitch.

"The coordinated customer–service team combined

with up-to-date CRM, will give us more data, more quickly on our customers. And provide us the information we need to understand our customers and resolve issues quickly.

"We already know that one-third of the complaints stem from customer delays and change requests. While our approach will be that the customer is always right—"

Brian and Mitch exchanged glances.

Kate looked at them intensely. "We also need to remind customers that delayed approvals delay production."

Brian crossed his arms across his chest.

"And we need to make post-sales calls to verify customer satisfaction. Our goal *must* be to go beyond customer satisfaction to customer delight. Think of the follow-up call as one more opportunity to build relationships, and scout out a new order.

"Richard, Debbie, and I are working on identifying other opportunities for improvement. We don't want anything falling through the cracks. So, if you notice an opportunity, please share it right away."

"Square deal," Brian said, showing interest.

Her staff appeared receptive at this point, as she had hoped. She cleared her throat before switching to sales practices. "Everyone in this room wants to improve our closing percentage, but we can only do that with a different strategy. We're using a standard transactional approach that's simple and familiar. But 'simple and familiar' hasn't delivered. We're not making our numbers, so we've got to change if we expect different outcomes. This requires a consultative sales strategy to identify what's driving a customer's decision-making and tailor a pitch that can close the sale. It's a small adjustment that'll deliver great results since it positions us on the customer's side.

"It means probing before presenting. Instead of leading with what we offer, we learn about the customer's pressing issues. We'll develop a series of questions to reveal their primary interests. This isn't rocket science. It's merely listening for your client's *current* priority and showing them how we can help them reach their goal. It's the basis for building a solid relationship."

Kate waited until Joann looked up from her tablet, then continued. "Online printers can't do that. Inexperienced salespeople can't do that. Firms with narrow product lines can't do that. But we can. And the sale will always go to the firm that can serve their customer's current interests.

"Given our large product portfolio, we can offer a multitude of solutions that will best serve each client. We won't start closing unless we're sure we've met their needs, whether that's price, quality, materials, or multiple needs. When a customer gives you vague requirements, clarify what they really want. Decipher what will furnish the client and us with outstanding results. We offer quality, design, and capacity that others can't come close to matching. But we have to let our customers know we're more than a typical printing firm. Engage in a conversation and then customize the pitch squarely at their priorities. Show the customer you're a knowledgeable partner and not just a vendor. Don't rush to close without digging deeper."

Mitch pumped his right knee up and down like a piston.

"Do you want to comment, Mitch?"

"Well. There are a lot of times customers can be turned off by a long pitch. They want you to show them what you have and make a quick decision. In and out."

"You're right. Sometimes a quick transaction is preferred. But most of the time, they'll be grateful you showed them a full range of options for their specific situation. We can't afford to be an "always-be-closing" transactional firm. That's the road to commoditization and low margins. It is much smarter to engage with the customer and learn about their needs. And even after the contract is signed, you can still collect a bit more information. Not for this sale but the next one.

"We need to keep our eyes on future sales too. Repeat business is always more cost-effective—and more enjoyable—than continually prospecting for new customers. Meeting customers' needs will build their loyalty to us and produce referrals. Word-of-mouth marketing is powerful, and consultative selling is the way to grow it.

"Look, Davis Printing has a good reputation, but we *can* make it better. We can become known as the best printer out there. We'll set ourselves apart from online and lower-margin players. I'm thrilled that's not our game. By building consultative relationships with our customers, we become a trusted resource. We can build the Davis brand into one that warrants loyalty, referrals, and testimonials. It'll pay off for all of us in the short- and long-term."

Despite the glowing description of these opportunities, Kate noticed that Brian was staring out the window. It wasn't long before he voiced his concerns.

"I have to say, this sounds like a lot of time visiting and talking with customers. When do we get down to business and *sell*?" he asked.

"You know selling is more than negotiating terms," Kate said. "I've sold on the golf course as well as over lunch and in the office. I bet you have too. Selling is a process. Of course, there are no guarantees. Sometimes it fails us. But how much time and effort does it take to make one cold call after another? How much time is wasted visiting with a customer who's dissatisfied with a past order? Shifting from a series of hit-or-miss transactions to building a following through consultative sales takes time, yes, but it's an investment that pays sizable dividends.

"Changing the way we work is uncomfortable, but imagine how it will *feel* to thrill your customers—not just sell them, but *thrill* them—*and* lift your commissions. We're going to work together to make that happen, and you'll see and feel the payoff—for you, the customer, and the company."

Kate took some time to let her passion sink in on the team. "I think it was Kenneth Elliott who said, 'The customer is not someone to argue with or match wits against—he is a person who brings us his wants. If we have sufficient imagination, we will endeavor to handle them effectively and profitably.'[1] That's the heart of consultative sales. We handle the customers' wants, and we benefit along with them."

After describing the advantages of a consultative strategy, Kate was ready to dig into specifics. "I've used Situational Mindsets for consultative sales, and it works. It uses six frames of reference to reveal a prospect's current business requirements or goals. No mind reading required. We ask questions to learn the client's pressing challenges and current realities. Getting a comprehensive picture reveals what is driving the customers so we can target the critical need. We can't rely on the information they gave us six months ago. We have to uncover what drives them now. Armed with that information, we tailor our proposal to spotlight the solutions that best meet their highest priority."

Mitch looked thoughtful—which, Kate noted, was encouraging. Joann smiled—as usual. But Brian's eyes rolled up. No matter. She pushed on.

"Situational Mindsets uses your talents in a different way. It directs your presentation to what's currently critical to the customer. We don't have to assume what *they* want based on what *most* customers order or on prior purchases. I've *seen* it work. Situational Mindsets nearly doubled sales for my team at MedSurgicals. This practice allowed us to speak the customer's language, hit their hot buttons, and zero in on their goals. We made more than a sale; we created loyal customers. We also crushed the competition and were highly rewarded for it.

"But things weren't always that way. Before we adopted that process, MedSurgicals stumbled badly after misreading the requirement for a huge, multi-location client. The loss of that account made us realize the high cost of not understanding the customer's current reality.

"We dropped the structured presentation. The canned approach was canned. Our salespeople were so used to mirroring a client's speech patterns and reading body language that, at first, some of us confused Situational Mindsets with personality variations or communication styles. Some wondered whether they would have to change their own personality, when all that was needed was to ask questions, analyze the responses, and steer the conversation toward how we could meet customer priorities.

"The new approach grabbed their attention. If we strayed into discussing products or features they weren't interested in, they got bored, and an opportunity was lost. Exploring what they cared about, presenting alternatives they hadn't considered, and preempting objections came from focusing on them and their interests—what they wanted and what they were trying to avoid. If they wanted something we couldn't give them, we told them the truth—and sometimes directed them to someone who could. That may sound like giving away business, but it built trust in our integrity, and we gained their loyalty. What we learned is that anytime you help a customer, you'll be rewarded. Maybe not today or tomorrow. But the payoff comes down the road. Eventually, they called *us* about upcoming purchase requests."

Brian shifted in his chair, reinforced the crease in his pants, and studied his loafers.

Kate opened her top left desk drawer, removed some notepads, and placed them on her desk. "For the next five minutes, would each of you list the frequent customer requests you get? I'll step out to give you time to reflect, and get us something to drink."

Kate stepped out of the room.

Five minutes later, she returned with four bottles of water and shared them with the team. "Okay, let me see what you came up with." She scanned the lists. "Excellent. These show how varied our customers' interests are. As you know, customers frequently give extensive *wants*, and it's our job to discover their driving *needs*." She set the papers on the table.

"Next, let's use what we know about our customers to see how Situational Mindsets helps us separate peripheral interests from critical needs. We have to detect what the core of the buying decision is currently, and we can do that with Situational Mindsets. A Mindset is a lens used to collect and analyze the customer's decision criteria. There are six Mindsets." Kate walked to the whiteboard and wrote *Inventing*.

"This is our first Mindset. It centers around unique offerings, creative designs, and original products and services."

Under *Inventing*, she added *Catalyzing*. "The Catalyzing Mindset is the one we use the most. It targets customer service, customization, commitment to total satisfaction, and responsiveness to customer requirements. This one highlights the importance of being willing to go to extremes to serve our customers."

"Let's move on to the next Mindset—*Developing*—which spotlights our internal capacity to handle large jobs, offer one-stop shopping, and provide flawless execution.

"The fourth area is *Performing*, and it also centers on internal issues. It prioritizes pricing, quality products, deadlines, delivery, and efficient, quality-controlled operations. This customer wants to know that we can reliably deliver steak as well as sizzle.

"The next Mindset is *Protecting.* This one addresses the customer's preference for a reputable brand, a firm with corporate integrity, a strong warranty, a respected member of the community, and a firm with bench strength. Customers check our website, the Better Business Bureau, online reviews.

"The final Mindset is *Challenging*, where customers want to work with a firm that shares industry trends and keeps them abreast of change. With a Challenging orientation, they'll check for eco-friendly processes, trends, and the opportunity to create a long-term partnership.

"Most customers operate with one or two of these Mindsets at a time. While everyone dreams of focusing on all six, no one has the resources—either the personnel or finances—to juggle them all simultaneously. Multitasking organizational goals is a myth. Choices must be made and adjusted as events warrant and realities change. The term Situational Mindsets reflects the importance of addressing new realities, whether through a different product line, expanded capacity, or customized service. The decision maker's frame of mind has established a goal. We have to understand what that is and meet it. A client with an end-of-year budget surplus will make different choices than one whose budget is in the red. Priorities change as situations shift. As soon as one goal is achieved, customers pivot to another aspiration or priority.

"*Current* is always the keyword because even with long-standing customers—people you know very well—thoughts and priorities swing to the newest challenge or opportunity. That impacts their buying criteria. We need to understand *their* point of view.

"Now consider your experience with customer requirements." Kate looked over the lists again. "Delivery is a major issue. Where do you think that would fall within the Situational Mindsets framework?"

Joann said, "I would classify it as the Performing Mindset because it's a reliability and specification factor dealing with execution."

"Right." Kate looked at the list again. "As you also noted, some customers want our design services for fresh, customized printing. What Mindset would that fall into?"

Mitch looked up suddenly. "Inventing, right?"

"Yep, you got it," Kate said.

She reviewed the other selling points, hearing only from Joann and Mitch, then asked, "From your experience, is anything that you listed *not* covered by one of the Mindsets?"

"Actually"—Joann paused—"no."

Mitch turned toward Joann, rested his hand on the edge of Kate's desk holding his list, and nodded. "Situational Mindsets captures them all."

Kate opened her folder and pulled out copies of a Situational Mindsets chart. "Here's a summary for our use." She handed them out.

SITUATIONAL MINDSET	PRIORITY	DESIRED OUTCOME	BENEFIT PITCH
Inventing	Industry Leader, Cutting-edge Products	Distinctive Products, Creative Designs	• Unique Offerings • Design Services • Exclusive Product Line
Catalyzing	Fast Growth, Strong Market Position, Expand Customer Base	Customer Focus, Customer Service, Responsive, Flexible	• Customer Centric • Dedicated to Customer Service & Satisfaction • Customized Service • Online Ordering and Tracking • Excellent Customer Reviews
Developing	Organization Structure, Integrated Systems, Aligned Goals, Effective Policies, Accountability	Capacity, Excellence, Flawless Operations	• One-stop Shopping • Outstanding Track Record, • Stable and Reliable, • Capacity for large jobs
Performing	Efficiency, ROI, Productivity, Effective Supply Chain, Efficiencies	Quality, Value, Guaranteed	• Quality Products • Value Pricing • On-time Delivery • Product Warranty • Efficient Operations
Protecting	High-performing Culture, Talented Workforce, Retention of Key Staff, Succession Planning, Employer of Choice, Engagement	Respected Brand, Solid Reputation, Trustworthy, Recognize as a "Good Place to Work"	• Reliable Brand • Corporate Integrity • Community Leader • Bonded • BBB A+ Rating • Talented, Committed Employees
Challenging	Seize Opportunities, Strategic Planning, Effective Business Model, Strategic Partnerships, Agility	Business Partners, Industry Knowledge, Sustainability, Supplier and Distributor Network	• Industry Knowledge, • Environmentally Friendly, • Sustainable Firm for Your Future, • Extensive Network

"This chart describes the Situational Mindsets, but remember, these are dynamic. If we assume a customer has a permanent Mindset, we won't succeed. Like us, customers change as circumstances change. You have noticed that customers change, haven't you?"

"All the time." Mitch laughed. "Had a high-end customer who was willing to pay for premium service, then on the next order negotiated like the money was coming out of his own pocket. Suddenly, it's price, price, price. Crazy."

"Right. Why do you think there was such a reversal?"

"He had a bad quarter, now he's counting pennies."

"That's why we have to check *every* time to understand what's driving the customer. It could be price one time and quality another. Expecting stable priorities is foolish, and so is thinking we need only one pitch. Customer interests are not static. Competition, technology, customers, and workforce are only a few of the factors they face, and these shape their thinking.

"There's a quote that we 'live in interesting times.' Some say it's from an old Chinese curse. *Interesting times* means having many changes and challenges.[2] We might think that if everything were stable, we would have an easier time. But change works in our favor too. Customers have to refresh their printed materials due to these changes. And when a customer hears about the products and services we offer, they may elect to upgrade the order. Those opportunities pop up also.

"It's up to us to customize our presentation to their present Mindset priority. I'd like everyone to come up with initial thoughts for each Mindset by Thursday. Then we'll edit them. I want to start using Situational Mindsets immediately. It'll take practice before you feel comfortable with it, but it won't take long for it to become second nature. Time spent inquiring and finding the right pitch yields great dividends down the road."

"But won't they resent being analyzed?" Mitch asked.

"We're not analyzing them. We're serving them. Mindsets address business issues, not people. Most people enjoy discussing their business and prefer tailored solutions. Clients don't want to feel that you're giving them a standard pitch hoping to score. Everyone enjoys being heard and feeling that they're getting special attention. Regardless of how you process the information, you're *listening.* And the greatest honor you can give anyone is listening to them and helping them achieve their goals.

"Before we end today, I have one more topic to discuss. Joann will be our point person as we look to expand our digital footprint. Tom and I have asked her to take the lead in winning online business. A strong digital presence won't substitute for personal relationships or on-site calls, but it'll enhance our brand and reach, especially for larger B2B work.

"Customers judge us on our digital presence as well as our products and services. Right now, our online impression is weak. Our website is outdated and doesn't list all of our product lines and services. Updating will showcase more of those. And we'll continue finding ways to streamline our operations."

"Huh?" Brian asked a bit loudly.

"What all of that means," Kate said, "is that we can leverage technology so we'll reduce administrative time and stand out from our competition. For example, if we can track our customers' internal proof timelines and give them a way to track their orders online, it will be a win-win. And, of course, it will reduce the number of calls to customer service—and to each of you—about late deliveries. Look, if the US Postal Service can provide tracking, well, it should be a cinch for us."

Joann smiled broadly, but Brian's face was set, his foot tapping the floor. Mitch glanced furtively at Brian and crossed his legs. It didn't take Sherlock Holmes to identify that the two of them were concerned. Brian certainly wasn't buying into these modifications. Kate wondered if he felt he was losing his senior status or that there would be less emphasis on field sales. Or was he concerned these changes signaled cost cutting and that he would take the first hit as the highest-paid salesperson? Whatever the reason, he would need help to make the transition.

"While we're addressing online sales, field sales are still our mainstay," Kate said. "We'll keep our focus on personalized customer service but stay alert for ways to improve and ways we can grow our business."

Mitch piped up. "Is *Tom* on board with all these

changes? He's never talked about online sales or technology before."

"Yes, he fully supports the CRM software and wants to see what we can accomplish online. If technology streamlines operations and increases sales, he'll support additional improvements. He truly wants to build the business through *all* sales channels. He sees the value of these initiatives, and I think you will too."

"I'm just not convinced there's value," Brian said. "'Situational Mindsets' sounds impressive, but nothing's really different, is it? After all, *everyone* wants the same thing: good value." The undertone was clear. Brian believed he knew this business better than Kate, a newcomer, and did not want to change.

Kate responded thoughtfully. "Well, Brian, I'm confident you'll see how effective Situational Mindsets and consultative sales when you zero in on what's top of mind for the customer. When you talk about their goals, you gain their business and build a relationship. I'm sure you'll master this quickly. And I'm here to help you and the entire team wherever I can. Everyone wants to succeed, and I know we will."

8

Pitfalls and Promises

Three weeks after Kate introduced Situational Mindsets and initiated consultative sales, she headed into an executive team meeting in Tom's office. At her first management meeting, she had seen him stash a bottle of Tums in his desk drawer just before it began. Lately, he no longer pulled out that drawer or massaged his temples as the prelude to interrupting someone. He was definitely more comfortable and open to new ideas.

Richard had told her these meetings were torturous in the past—a minefield of complaints and resentments, with Tom lobbing surprises to show he was on top of events and rumors. Tom had not hidden his frustration with current events. But he was not alone. Everyone was concerned with their turf instead of the firm's success. Recently, though, tension and complaints had subsided. Now information was exchanged, and collaborative problem-solving surfaced. People arrived prepared with solutions rather than a litany of complaints. Kate hoped this trend would continue.

Tom was seated at his desk, which was more organized than Kate had ever seen it. Richard and Debbie arrived behind her, discussing the anticipated reopening of SoHo next month.

"Good morning," Tom said. "I brought some coffee and donuts for us today. Help yourselves, and we'll get started."

Kate walked to the credenza for a glazed donut and some coffee, smiling since this was the first time refreshments had been offered. Richard and Debbie snatched up the chocolate donuts. Once everyone was settled, Tom distributed the monthly financial reports.

"The numbers are looking up," he said. "As you can see, we've had a reduction in overtime, improved sales, and a drop in accounts receivable." He smiled.

Debbie spoke up. "The improvement in AR could be connected to a drop in customer complaints. I'm happy to say the customer-service team plus cross-functional collaboration make a difference." She smiled. "We're not entirely where I'd like to be, but we're improving all the time."

"Great," Tom said. "Keep it up." He turned to Kate. "Next update."

Kate said, "The sales team is hustling, and we have some very promising opportunities. Our online platform is still evolving, but we have solid expectations in the short-term."

Richard finished his coffee and set the cup on the floor. "We've handled the uptick well. Having fewer rush orders has smoothed our schedule. But equipment maintenance cost has bumped up."

As the updates continued, Tom added little except an occasional "good to know" or "glad to hear it." He was listening *here* rather than scouting for information out on the shop floor.

When the discussion came to a lull, Tom's gaze wandered from face to face. "I'm impressed with our progress. The teamwork since the explosion has transferred to our operation. And if we build on it, that will make a difference for us now and into the future."

Kate noticed that Tom had swung from a sole focus on numbers, which was characteristic of the Performing Mindset, toward the Challenging Mindset's future focus. A welcomed shift. Fixating on short-term gains for too long in a dynamic industry was risky.

Digital transformation and commoditization were sweeping the printing industry along. The future was closer than it looked, and preparation was critical. Time to bring up the redheaded stepchild.

"With our future in mind," Kate said, "Joann has made good headway with our digital platform, and we've started using a consultative relationship selling strategy. I think it's time for me to draft a comprehensive marketing plan for us to review. I can use this team's input to tailor it so that we effectively capture opportunities."

"Seems a little early," Tom said. "The CRM trial isn't over, and we're just getting things in gear."

"I agree. However, we must continue to boost our brand and build momentum. Before long, I expect we'll have higher volume, so it's smart to have a plan locked down and ready to launch. Preparing for the best-case outcome makes sense."

"I suppose there's no harm in considering options," Tom said. "But it has to be realistic about the level of funding we can afford. We aren't ready for a huge investment. We just aren't there yet."

"I hear you," Kate said, recognizing his Performing Mindset. "We can select what's feasible in the short run that will also support our longer-term goals."

"That's the spirit!"

Excellent, Kate thought. Tom had not rejected the idea outright. She could not push him *too* hard, but planning always paid off, especially as things started moving. Momentum was magical for both customers and employees. Keeping things on track was worth the effort.

She would solicit input from her team, listen to the

customers, and check the competition. Building a major marketing plan was of no use unless it was feasible, and the team committed to executing it.

•

At the next Sales meeting, Joann enthusiastically reported that "the firm is on several vendor websites, including local, state, *and* federal government sites."

"So *that's* digital marketing?" Brian muttered with a sideways glance at Joann.

"It's part of building our online presence, yes—making us visible to potential customers. Though, I concede it isn't much yet."

"It's a terrific start, Joann," Kate interjected. "I'm working on a marketing plan to expand our brand and market scope across multiple channels. In the meantime, keep expanding our visibility." Kate turned to Brian and Mitch. "How is Situational Mindsets working for you? Any concerns, questions, issues?"

"To be honest," Mitch said, "I'm making an effort to gauge each customer's Mindset and current goals. I have good results asking about their priority. Inquiring about their interest has been well received. And I get a lot more information than when I'm leading them. I think it helps build rapport. But haven't landed a big account yet."

He was moving in the right direction. Good. In fact, Kate would have been suspicious if he had suddenly expressed booming enthusiasm.

"What about you?" she asked Brian.

"Oh, I haven't had the time. This situational stuff is the last thing on my mind. See ... well ... I've been concentrating on the deal with Alice Notley ... at First Light Stores ..."

"Yes, when do you expect to close? That 'deal' has been in the works for a few weeks." Brian had repeatedly sidestepped specifics on the timing.

"Well, it went south. Plain and simple. I can't believe it slipped away." He stared down at his hands as he rubbed his palms together.

Kate remained focused and objective. Maybe she could help. "What derailed it?"

"Who knows? Probably internal politics. I've worked with Alice a long time. It's—it was—a solid relationship. I knew what made her tick. But *something* must've happened. She cooled off out of the blue. Bottom line is, the deal is dead. I told Tom just before I came in. I'm not gonna be another Larry and bury bad news."

So far, the value of Situational Mindsets had not registered for Brian. He relied on his old habits and relationships with buyers rather than probing for *current* information so he could assess the *current* situation. Worse, when a deal cooled, he did not ask why, which was the hallmark of a transactional approach. That he had no clue how to get things back on track was worse. He must not let a good customer slip away. Kate also registered that he had told Tom about this loss before telling her. She decided to work with Brian one-on-one to dig into the details and discuss next steps.

"All right," she said, "I think we've covered the essentials today. Let's get back to the business of selling with outstanding service."

•

When her staff left and cleared the hall, Kate went to Tom's office, but not to throw Brian under the bus. She wanted Tom to understand her plan to work with Brian and ensure his commitment to consultative sales.

She found Tom at his desk, and he waved her in. "I just heard from Brian about the problem with First Light Stores," she said, "and he told me you know."

"Problem? I thought it was dead." Tom pushed his chair back from his desk.

"It may be, but I'm not sure. I'm not ready to write it off. I wish Brian had told me when he first felt resistance. We could've developed an alternative approach. But let's not write the obituary yet."

"He and I go back years, so we regularly keep each other up-to-date."

"I understand, but he's making the assumption the deal is dead when he doesn't know what drove the client's decision. We need to discover the issue and reestablish a solid relationship with them for future business. So far, I haven't heard anything that tells me the deal can't be revived. I'm not promising a turnaround. But I can promise that Brian and I will try to bring it back to life."

"Well, Kate, give it your best, but it's a long shot."

"I agree, but it won't be a shot in the dark. Situational Mindsets will help us determine what's driving this decision. At the very least, we'll get valuable intel on why we lost the bid. And the best case? We'll find a way to close the sale after all."

Tom looked up at Kate and nodded, his lips pressed together. "We do need to check out what happened, and I'm happy you'll team up with him to find out," he said. "Kate, I mean it. Give it a try. I don't expect miracles. I'd love to salvage this deal. While Brian has a great deal riding on this, we all do too. Hopefully, we can win this in the end."

"I'll keep you posted."

•

When Kate stopped by Brian's office, he sat facing the window with his back to the door.

"Brian." No response. "Brian," Kate said louder.

"Oh ... yeah." He turned to face her.

"Let's talk about First Light Stores. What do you think happened?"

"It's just dead."

"Okay, but how do you *know* that?"

"I *feel* it because my calls aren't being returned."

"But you don't *know* it? What do you think drove the decision?"

"What difference does it make? The contract's been lost."

"Well, if it is dead, we have nothing to lose from investigating why. If it isn't lost, we have everything to gain. Let's explore what could've turned a promising opportunity around. There might be a way to salvage it."

Brian grimaced, then tightly shut his eyes. He was obviously remorseful.

"Look, I'm not playing the blame game here. Think about your contacts with Alice and any changes within the organization that might've impacted her choice. We have to understand her Mindset and what drove her decision."

"I dropped the ball. And now, I don't want to raise hopes since there's only a slim chance we can win this."

"Nobody's pointing fingers. That's unproductive," Kate said. Brian often assigned blame, so he probably assumed others would resort to guilt trips too. And he might be concerned that her goal was to collect ammunition on his failure.

Kate laid out her thinking. "You know, this can be a test of Situational Mindsets. If we discover key information and make smart adjustments, we'll see if the practice will make a difference. Maybe it can. Maybe it can't. The point is, we're working in the dark. So, together, let's get Alice to share her priorities with us. We have nowhere to go but up."

Brian's mouth parted, his brow lifted. "Like I said, I've known her a long time. I assumed our relationship carried weight. I miscalculated."

"You weren't necessarily wrong. Even good friends

can say no when circumstances require it. Are you aware of any recent events at the firm? Is anything different?"

This time, instead of resisting and deflecting, Brian looked thoughtful. "Hmm. The order was much larger than anything they placed in the past. Their recent merger might've changed their needs. Their purchase order had more drop-off locations. And she had expressed concern about late deliveries on a prior order. But we didn't cause the problem. Their proof process has so many review levels that it threw a wrench into our schedule."

"Good insights. So, what likely drives their decisions now?"

"As a fast-growing firm, maybe speed is key." He stopped. "Ohhh, man ..."

"What is it?"

"You know, I was pitching price. Alice wasn't negotiating price at all. She focused on delivery." He pulled out the chart she had given him and looked at it. "I guess she prioritized Catalyzing—speed over price! *That's* her driver right now."

"I think you're right." Kate nodded slowly. "Let's dig in. What do you know about late-delivery incidents?"

"There've been more than a few." His brow wrinkled.

"Enough to damage our reputation in their eyes?"

"Maybe," he said, "especially if speed is their primary concern."

"If she's working from the Catalyzing Mindset, she has to be confident that we'll keep to our schedules. That she can count on us. Let's develop a proposal that builds that confidence. We could guarantee a healthy discount for any delay so she knows there's no way we'll fail to produce on time."

"Smart," Brian said. "Will Production okay that?"

"Let's find out."

•

"Could we have a word with you?" Kate asked as she and Brian stopped at Richard's office door that afternoon.

"Sure." He waved them in. "Have a seat."

"Thanks," Kate said. "We'll try to keep it brief. We have a situation we want to run by you."

After a glance around the office, Brian sat beside her. "Yes. Well, I've been working for weeks to land a big sale with First Light Stores."

Richard nodded. "That *is* a good one."

"They've been ordering from us for years. I thought we were about to close and"—Brian lifted his right hand and gestured to the side—"she changes her mind. No deal. We think the issue might be delivery speed."

"Brian and I want to propose a guaranteed delivery schedule with the assurance of a discount if we're late," Kate said.

"This is our best shot at salvaging this sale, as well as the account," Brian added. "But it'll impact you, so we wanted your support for this special client."

"I know they're a good long-standing customer, and we don't want to lose them," Richard said. "I'm getting ready to implement what I call 'Plan B.' It means outsourcing to trade shops when we're swamped in-house. It's worth it to win this business until we can increase our capacity. When you finalize the specs, let me know, and I'll do whatever I can to give you what you need."

"Oh," Brian said. "Uh, okay. And I'll see if there's an option for partial delivery to minimize the impact on Production."

"Great." Kate smiled at Richard's support. "Thanks for the cooperation. We'll get back to you, and hopefully, we can seal the deal. We're going to do all we can to make First Light Stores a loyal customer."

As Kate and Brian walked back to Sales, she asked, "What will get us face time with Alice Notley?"

After a moment, Brian's face lit up. "*You*," he said.

"I'll use your arrival as the purpose of a visit. I'll introduce you as our new honcho. I'm sure she'll want to meet you. And we can develop a pitch in advance that'll address her Catalyzing Mindset."

"Great idea!"

•

A week later, they sat in Alice's office, facing her chrome-and-black desk in azure-blue molded-plastic chairs that were ... surprisingly comfortable. "Brian is our top salesman," Kate said with a smile. "I've heard great things about you and First Light's fast growth."

Alice pushed her blunt-cut blonde hair back from her tanned face. "He mentioned you recently joined Davis Printing?"

"Yes, I did. I'm going to let Brian tell you about the changes we're making to serve our customers. We think these modifications will improve on our outstanding customer service."

"Thanks, Kate." Brian sat forward. "It's exciting, really. With improved tracking software and streamlined inside communications, we're better able to service our customers, including guaranteed delivery dates."

Alice lifted her chin a bit and smiled.

"I realize First Light Stores is expanding its operations," Brian said, "and we want to partner with you to meet all of your printing needs. As you know, we're committed to exceptional customer service, quality, value, and *timely* deliveries. And we'll guarantee everything in writing."

"Brian, thanks for telling me about these changes. Actually, it's great news. Our growth means we are increasingly relying on our providers. We've adopted a no-surprise standard as a result. I'll send you the specs this afternoon, and I look forward to seeing a proposal and the guarantees." Alice stood and extended her hand.

"I'll work on terms I'm sure will more than satis-fy your requirements," Brian said as he shook her hand. "We appreciate the opportunity to work with you."

•

The following two months produced more sales. Kate's department was meeting its targets, and the pipeline was full. Pleased with the progress, she happily updated the management team. "After resurrecting First Light Stores to a living whale, the impact and value of using a con-sultative Situational Mindsets approach have been firm-ly established with everyone on the team." She grinned broadly.

"Great to hear." Tom pounded his desk.

Kate continued. "I'm sure you've all noticed that the wrinkles between Production and Sales have dissolved."

The others nodded to that assessment.

"Sales continues to win bids. We've upsold a variety of special finishes, as well as design services. Online, we're citing the advantages of a brick-and-mortar printer and offering local on-site calls for special projects. That's bringing in fresh leads. Follow-up sales visits for those have reaped more business, thanks to the new sales ap-proach. We're getting compliments and referrals. Things are going well."

"The numbers certainly match your assessment," Tom said.

So, he *had* been keeping track. Kate had noticed he was not walking the halls as frequently to "see how things are going." Yet another sign of progress. Things were moving in the right direction.

•

Sales continued to grow, with larger corporate and insti-tutional clients. Joann landed a major contract with the

Government Printing Office (GPO), which was privatizing more work. To Kate's delight, that long-term contract motivated Tom to fund a limited marketing campaign. Displaying exceptional collaboration, Sales, Production, and design (which operated within Production) creatively worked to close two large bids.

For the first time in ages, Sales beat revenue goals. Client calls were more productive. The whole team had impressed customers with the company's ability to provide high-quality, reliable service and customized solutions. Consultative sales also provided the opportunity to highlight various products and services. Business was flowing, but as with any good news, ramifications occurred.

The increased business stretched Production's staff and equipment. "Too much business is a *good* problem to have," Richard good-naturedly quipped to Kate one day, "but the pressure can't be ignored for long, or cracks will appear."

Wanting to avoid major trouble, they jointly approached Tom about the overload. Tom approved additional outsourcing for some of the customized projects, but Kate and Richard made it clear that was an interim step. The long-term solution was to expand Production. Tom agreed and said that he would authorize the equipment after another quarter of growth. He was planning for the future. And it was bright.

9

Strategy and Renewal

As Kate walked across the production floor for her weekly meeting with Richard, employees were hustling, and all the machines were in operation. She had seen this level of activity before, and despite appearance, order existed in what others may assume was turmoil.

Iraq. Yes, this resembled a command center in Camp Liberty at the height of the surge—continuous, intense activity, perpetual urgency, everyone in motion. This level of maximum effort was not a sustainable pace.

"What's going on out there?" she asked as she entered Richard's office.

"Out there? Business as usual ... at least lately. It's what we talked about, Kate. The upsurge in sales is really stretching Production."

"To the breaking point?"

"No, no, not quite yet, but we certainly need more staff and equipment. In the short run, I've got to bite the bullet and outsource overflow."

They discussed the amount of work and the cost of farming out jobs to a trade shop.

"Richard, we should take this to Tom, don't you think? We need to keep our customers happy, but we also have to think about the staff. Supplementing with trade shops will send a message to Tom that you need additional staff and equipment." She glanced back at the work area. "We can't afford to burn out our people or lose them due to this pace."

"Right. But let's start slow—asking for two additional staff—and then move on to the equipment issues. Once we've reached a sustainable profit, he'll approve capital investments."

"Well then, let's ask him for two positions and plant the seeds for equipment. We should act immediately on outsourcing and staffing to meet customer expectations as well as your staff's."

"Sounds like a plan. Let's see if he's available."

•

Tom looked happy to see Kate and Richard come in. They presented the issues and their proposed solutions. Richard cited the need for more equipment, given Kate's growth projections.

"I hope you didn't expect an immediate rejection," Tom said. "But you know you won't get an unqualified, immediate approval, right?" He grinned. "I'm very pleased with our sales growth, internal cooperation, and better cash flow. You've both done a great job, and we need to keep our customers happy, so we can't let schedules slip." He leaned back in his chair. "For now, let's outsource what we can't handle to the trade shops but keep a close eye on the bottom line. And, of course, keep me in the loop. I'll back you up by approving *one* new hire as soon as you find the right fit. As for the rest, let's watch the financials and revisit staffing and equipment upgrades down the road."

"Fair enough, thanks," Richard said. He turned to leave.

Kate followed him into the hallway. "That went well," she said. "It won't be long. We have the momentum going for us, and great results will follow."

"I'm pleased Tom came through," Richard said. "Short-term relief and maybe more later—he's trusting our judgment. That feels good."

"It *does*. His priorities are changing too."

•

Kate checked in with Debbie about plans that were being evaluated by the customer service team.

"Between our team handling the incoming issues and Sales and Production preventing issues from arising, we've turned a corner." Debbie patted a small stack of folders on her desk. "These are all the complaints I've got. I used to be swamped."

"Sure beats the let-sleeping-dogs-lie philosophy," Kate said.

"And the if-it-ain't-broke-don't-fix-it philosophy too." Debbie chuckled.

"Can you or the team pull together a report that documents complaint volume, resolutions, costs, and outcomes? Although we're monitoring issues, we may be overlooking patterns that might lead to other opportunities to improve customer relations."

"Perfect. By the way, besides having fewer customer complaints, we've received some nice notes attached to incoming checks. The best news"—Debbie's eyes reflected her smile—"is the increasing number of excellent reviews online. Joann showed me several. I pulled together a packet of some of these and was planning to shoot it over to you and Richard to share with your teams. Needless to say, Tom gets one too."

"Great idea! I'd love to celebrate good results to show that we're on the right track."

•

The next day, Tom stopped in at Kate's office. "I've got

a copy of the positive customer reviews here. I can't tell you how pleased I am. You and Richard deserve a great deal of credit. The interaction between the two of you— between *all* of you—is the best it's ever been at Davis Printing." He sat on a chair in front of her desk. "Sales have taken off, and I'm confident we're running on all cylinders now. But be patient with me a little longer on other changes. I want to think about the long term to ensure all of our actions are aligned. It's time to focus on our future."

"That's exciting."

"You know, I've always wanted to grow the business. I just never felt the time was right until now. I've been at the mercy of events, but that's not smart, and it won't produce a sustainable strategy."

"Don't you think that's a bit harsh?" Kate raised her eyebrows and smiled slightly.

"No, I don't. I've been playing the short game, a game of whack-a-mole. The team is doing an excellent job handling the day-to-day routine. It's time for me to concentrate on our strategy for our future. Of course, I'll need input from everyone. And to that end, I'm scheduling a planning session to kick off a strategy review to consider options for our future."

"Count me in. Richard and I have been bouncing around some ideas about staffing, systems improvements, efficiency, and marketing ourselves under a bigger umbrella that can capture larger, upscale clients. Also, expanding our prepress services would be a smart move. We could become a go-to printer with a design shop integrated."

"I'm open to ideas, but only as part of a unified business strategy. We need to put everything on the table to guarantee alignment and success. We must have a feasible, comprehensive plan."

Kate tapped her chin with her pen. "It would be good

to agree on our *current* state first, including our strengths and shortcomings. It could be the foundation for an effective plan to move forward."

"Sounds good. We'll start there."

•

Kate and Richard consulted Debbie and some key customers to gain valuable input. They also met with Production and Sales to gain their perspectives. The production staff expressed deep reservations about accelerating demand without more staff and equipment.

Richard asked Kate to meet a few days later to discuss their findings. "Hey, happy to tell you the new press assistant is working out well," Richard said. "Having that added operator is great, but it won't be enough. There just aren't enough people or presses."

Kate frowned. "It's hard to think about the future with that short-term pressure."

"We could increase overtime—temporarily—in order to meet demand, at least until after we have the bigger picture. But it's got to be voluntary *and* short term, or there might be trouble. The staff needs to see light at the end of the tunnel."

"Definitely. Would this be more cost-effective than sending work to a trade shop?"

"Yes, as long as I don't lose employees. If I have to hire and train lots of people, it'll set me way back. Then I'd face lower productivity, delayed deliveries, and unacceptable stress. I expect there'll be enough volunteers since it's short term."

•

Richard called an all-hands Production meeting and invited Kate. He stood tall as he addressed his staff. "Sales have been good, but it also means more work for us."

A few groans emanated from the group.

Richard proceeded anyway. "Kevin's been a great help at the press since he joined us, but we still can't keep up. Tom's approved overtime as a makeshift solution. It won't be forever, and it will be voluntary. While the overtime means fatter paychecks, I recognize that not everyone wants the strain. Again, any overtime will be temporary and *voluntary*. Everyone's needs will be accommodated."

A short redheaded woman raised her left hand, and her left eyebrow. "And you're sure it'll remain *voluntary*."

"Guaranteed," he said. "We all deserve reasonable work hours. And Tom recognizes the need to make some changes. He's developing a strategy to ensure a promising future for Davis Printing. And underlying our plans is the goal of creating a sustainable work-life balance. For now, we have to cover the immediate gaps that come with growth. Can I get a quick sense of how many of you will consider signing up for some extra hours? Just raise your hand."

Several hands went up immediately.

•

A week later, the executive team met to assess trends and consider their future. Tom asked Kate to report first on emerging customer requirements.

"A number of clients are asking for specialty items," she said. "Product labels, printing for promotional items for trade-show bags, convention-booth giveaways, signage for conventions and shows, even logos for branded shirts.

"I reviewed these with Richard to see which are the most viable. Product labels are fairly easy to produce, but others require a detailed analysis including projected investment and margins. We're both eager for Davis Printing to become a one-stop shop to build customer loyalty.

But each new product line needs to be evaluated for its potential contribution to our long-term growth and financial health."

Kate sat up straighter and summarized the issues. "Are they worth the investment? Do they offer reasonable barriers to prevent competitors from poaching on them? What can we handle in-house? Should we consider partnering on some products? For instance, we could work with a clothing manufacturer to expand our offerings and become a true one-stop print shop."

She glanced at each of them. "So, I'm asking: Do we feel it's wise to research these opportunities? If so, I'm happy to start the process and present some background on what it will take, what it will cost, and whether it would be feasible."

"I'm all for it." Debbie nodded. "We should get a handle on the facts first."

"And evaluate each potential product line and niche separately," Richard said.

Tom weighed in last. "Kate, why don't you perform your due diligence and get back to us."

"Will do." Kate hoped her next remarks would be as well received. "Now, let me turn to the issue of social media marketing. As you know, Joann has rapidly expanded our online presence, and she's proved its mettle. Sales has reached the point where we should consider hiring another inside salesperson."

"I see." Tom sat forward. "Any other expenses I should consider while we're in the planning stages?"

Richard bit. "Actually, you already have my request to fund an additional shift. And we can't put off the installation of a large-format digital press any longer. We're being outgunned by shops with bigger presses. We can't continue losing ground to them."

"You know I'm leery about taking on debt. That said"—Tom took a deep breath—"new lines of business are essential to our future. We can't become stagnant in our fast-changing industry. I want to expand, to grow, but let's manage the risk carefully. I have two minds: I want growth but without unnecessary risk, and I don't want to spend money to chase fads. Our strategy needs to be based on solid data and business model."

This was a classic tug-of-war, not between two minds but two Mind*sets*. On one end of the rope was Tom's Catalyzing Mindset, which viewed risk as necessary for reward. On the other end was his strong Performing Mindset, which strived to reduce risk and ensure profitability. Kate felt as if she were watching a suspense thriller—live and in person. Which one would win? What would he do next?

"So ..." Tom turned his pen around in his hands. "I've got to strike the right balance for our future. Starting Davis Printing was a risk, and it paid off. And I want it to thrive long into the future. Here's what I think we should do. We need to investigate, vigorously"—he gave each of them a determined look—"what constitutes an acceptable level of risk for our future. There's no gain without some pain, but I want to mitigate negative surprises as much as possible. It's fine to talk about going for broke, except for the part about actually going broke."

Their chuckling eased the seriousness that had built in the room.

He continued. "I confess that my nose-to-the-grindstone manner has probably curtailed opportunities. I've always believed that working hard pays off—and I still do—but working smarter delivers better dividends. A static, dogged approach won't succeed in this dynamic industry. Digital will only grow, and we can't adopt a path toward commoditization and its low profit margins. We can do better, especially since we have the talent we need. We've got to look at our business from the ground level, the five-thousand-foot level, and from fifty thousand feet. Then we'll achieve sustainable, profitable growth."

His changing priorities gratified Kate. She welcomed Tom's challenge to think beyond current concerns. He was now willing to test assumptions and explore alternatives, which reflected the Challenging Mindset.

On a roll, Tom continued. "But I can't afford to be flying blind, either. Thanks to all of you, I don't have to. To give ourselves time to think, let's get together tomorrow and explore our options. We need to do serious number crunching and risk analysis before we leap into social-media marketing, adding a production shift, or purchasing a large-format press. Kate, please involve Joann in this effort."

"That would be great." Kate had one more suggestion. "You know, Sales is using Situational Mindsets to collect and evaluate our clients' realities. It prevents us from missing critical aspects. Brian turned around the First Light Stores deal once he fully evaluated Alice Notley's situation. He's now a convert to the practice." She hoped this example would encourage Tom and the entire team to examine where the firm stood and where opportunities lay.

"You might be wondering what this has to do with strategic planning. As a company, we can use the six Mindsets to collect relevant internal and external information for our planning process realities. We'll be able to identify our prospects and our potential risks."

Richard shifted in his chair. "What do you mean by 'internal and external realities'?"

"Internal realities deal with our workforce, process and policies. This would include questions such as: Do we have the right skills? Do we have a succession plan to replace retirees? Will our current facilities and equipment meet our future needs? External factors include competitive trends, governmental regulations, upgrades in technology, and the economy. By viewing all the pieces in play, we can weigh possible gains against risks."

Tom leaned forward. "Like being overly optimistic and making inappropriate investments."

"Certainly. And Situational Mindsets would also help us analyze our organizational life cycle to validate where we are and ensure our next steps are feasible." Kate let that thought ruminate in their minds, then continued.

"Cycles are common in business, of course—product life cycles, project life cycles, budgeting cycles, and so on. Organizations have life cycles, too, and each stage presents different strengths and constraints.

"The issues we concentrate on when we start a project vary significantly from those when the project is running smoothly or when it closes. The same is true in organizations, which progress through stages. Discussing and agreeing on our current cycle stage allow us to pinpoint our key priorities and vital issues. When we confirm where we are, we can factor the priorities of the next stage into our planning.

"We either evolve or wither. Being out of touch with reality kills far more businesses than competitive pressure or adverse legislation—or other typically cited reasons. Consider names like Polaroid, Eastern Airlines, Lehman Brothers, and Blockbuster—they were *household names*. Well, until they weren't. Yet they suffered because they failed to deal effectively with changing realities. As a result, each of them has paid a high price.

"You know what else they have in common? Every one of them stuck to outdated assumptions and business models. Agility is not merely an advantage. It's as essential to an organization as oxygen is to humans."

Kate stood and picked up the remote to a projector she had set up. "I'd like to share a chart to illustrate the life cycle of an organization and how each stage corresponds to a Situational Mindset." She clicked the remote and projected the chart on the wall.

LIFE CYCLE STAGE	CONCERN	MINDSET
Birth or Rebirth	New Products and Services	Inventing
Growth	Sales, Market Share and Customer Service	Catalyzing
Stature	Infrastructure, Policies, Facilities and Planning	Developing
Prime	Efficiencies, Quality, Budget and ROI	Performing
Mature	Culture, Engagement, and Talent	Protecting
Renewal	Trends, Opportunities, Strategy and Alliances	Challenging

"In the left column are the organizational life-cycle stages. The middle column captures the concerns dominating each stage, and the right-hand column identifies the corresponding Situational Mindsets. Whether we look at the right or left column, the factors in the middle need to be covered. I believe Davis Printing has progressed from its entrepreneurial roots into a well-established firm and that we're likely entering the Renewal stage—looking to the future, refining our business model, and discovering fresh opportunities.

"Tom, this is putting you on the spot since I just presented the idea, but where would you agree?"

"It won't be the first time you've challenged me," he half-jokingly said.

Several seconds passed as he studied the slide. "Okay, here it is. As I see it, we've been in Growth and Stature. However, the acceleration of printing technology has spawned more business models. That indicates we need to *start* thinking about Renewal." After another pause, he turned to Kate. "Is it feasible to jump over two stages?"

Richard and Debbie laughed, and Tom soon joined in.

"If it's our priority right now, then we concentrate on it. Jumping two stages will require more-effective planning and communication than if we moved one stage forward. Does everyone agree that we need a major strategic review to position us for the future?"

"I'm on board with a strategic thrust," Richard said.

Debbie patted the arm of her chair. "As am I."

"Glad to hear"—Kate grinned—"However …"

Tom sighed. "Uh-oh …"

Kate continued. "However, though we've agreed about what we're focusing on, we can't overlook the issues connected with all the stages. For example, if we develop a plan and ignore adjusting the infrastructure, policies, and responsibilities that are part of the Stature stage and the Developing Mindset, we'll fail. They form the *foundation* to implement a new strategy. Too many organizations develop a great vision but fail to align their systems to turn their plan into reality. Outdated internal policies, structure, and systems can cripple a new approach. Everything must be aligned to achieve success. So, as we plan for major strides forward, we've got to create an environment where it will succeed. Handling both at the same time will be a challenge, especially since we have to do all that while operating within our *current* business plan. It's like replacing a tire on a moving car. But I think we can maintain a dual focus: building our current business and targeting other business avenues."

"I see that." Tom looked at the slide. "I can see us addressing the Prime and Mature stages, as well as focusing on"—he read from her slide—" 'efficiencies, quality, and profit' and then on to 'culture, engagement, and development.' So, all the stages are important because all the Mindsets are. I get it. The Developing Mindset aligns with the Stature stage, and that does require attention now. 'Infrastructure, policy, facilities, and resources' are what you and Richard and I have been talking a lot about lately. So, I see that factors under Stature, along with the Challenging Mindset, shape strategic success, right?"

"Right."

"Sort of a chicken-or-egg issue, isn't it? Which comes first?" Tom, again on a roll, rolled on. "The Developing Mindset under the Stature stage needs to support our strategy. But we can't let ourselves get stuck on that. First, we need to target strategic planning so our business continues to thrive. Then we can devise the infrastructure, policies, and facilities to make it happen."

Tom took a breath. "Let me remind you why I founded this company in the first place. Thirty years ago, I saw an opportunity for growth in the printing industry. The need for printing had increased as the importance of marketing grew along with the number of small businesses. As established firms outsourced more of their printing, I grabbed that opportunity. It was a wonderful challenge, and I loved every minute of being an entrepreneur.

"However, over the years, I held on to the day-to-day activities instead of continuing to search for opportunities. When technology started competing with traditional printing firms, I kept my focus on the day to day instead of looking toward the future. The marketplace was changing, but instead of keeping up, I dug into internal issues. I tried to micromanage, and the firm's outlook suffered." He sighed.

"Well, those days are over," he said. "I'm excited to plan for our future. The prospect of finding new opportunities rekindles the old entrepreneurial spirit. We're going to pursue exciting possibilities that match our mission. We'll probably confront some challenges, but as a team, we'll handle them."

"That sounds great." Kate was nodding. "And I agree that we'll succeed with whatever comes our way, as long as we keep an eye on our realities and priorities."

"We must," Tom said. "Strategy without implementation is a fantasy. Enticing but illusory. We can't expect smooth sailing on every front, but together we can handle the bumps in the road effectively. So, let's get started."

Tom pulled out his schedule book. "Let's set up a full-day strategy session to kick off our journey toward revitalizing and renewing our operations. To prep for the session, I want each of us to prepare a SWOT analysis of what's promising and what's dangerous. Based on these insights, we can catalog our internal strengths and weaknesses as well as external opportunities and threats. With this underpinning, we devise a promising, practical strategic plan.

"I think our analysis should focus on the next two years." He tapped the top of his notebook. "Now, you may think we should focus on five years, but that's an eternity, given our digitally driven industry. With accelerating technology and competition, two years is the wisest window for now."

Kate recognized that Tom had balanced his Challenging Mindset and its focus on capturing the dynamic state of the industry with his Performing Mindset's practical concern for managing risk by not overshooting what was doable. He would only make significant investments if they supported a solid, workable plan. Aspirations excite and offer great promise, but for Tom, aspirations had to be grounded by levelheaded analysis and vigilant planning. He was ensuring the best of both.

10

The Bottom Line

Sam Meyers, the owner of SoHo, gave Kate a warm handshake when she reached the reservation stand. "My favorite customer," he said, as always. Apparently, Tom and Richard were his "favorite customers" too, but she didn't mind. Sam was her favorite restaurateur.

After the restaurant reopened, she had eaten there many times, and she had reserved a room for a holiday celebration. When she arrived early for the event, she found that silver and gold had exploded inside. Shiny silver garlands framed the doorways, decorated with golden balls, tall white poinsettias sat in every corner, and red poinsettias adorned the tables. She smiled at Sam. "The place looks incredible."

"My wife." He pointed to his left, where Connie was laying a platter of cookies on one of the tables. "She's the decorator." He handed Kate a small wrapped gift. "For later. Just a token for the season. Please, go in and enjoy the party. I'll be here all night. If I can be of any assistance, just let me know."

"Thank you, Sam. Everything looks perfect, as always."

In the dining area, all of the tables had been moved along the walls to form serving tables. Brian and his wife, Valerie, stood near the dessert table to the right, sampling the cookies.

"So good to see you both here tonight." Kate shook Valerie's hand, then Brian's. "How are things at the shop, Valerie?"

"It's the bakery's busy season. I hired seasonal help to get all of the cakes done."

"Ohh"—Kate looked at the sheet cake on the table behind Valerie. It was decorated with the Davis logo above a detailed picture of the printing plant—"did you make that one? It's fantastic!"

"We did. One of my workers specializes in replicas. She's really good."

"I'll say." Kate picked up a sugar cookie from one of the platters. "Brian, may I intrude on the holiday and ask if we could move our Monday-afternoon meeting to ten a.m.? Let's put our heads together on that international-banking client."

"Sure. That's fine. I've got things ready." He gave her a thumbs-up.

Kate spied the punch bowl. "Well, enjoy the party. I'm heading over to get something to drink."

She crossed the room to the black-tiled bar and accepted a glass from the bartender. "Happy holidays," she said, then turned to stroll about.

To the left were five tables where people had seated themselves with their plates. At the second table, Mitch and Joann were laughing their way through a discussion about holiday trivia. Kate's team had pulled together well. She nodded to Ken from Production as she passed on her way to get cookies.

She had finished her cookie, so she stopped at the fruit display. She poked a small strawberry with a wooden skewer, passed it under the chocolate fountain beside the fruit, and enjoyed.

Debbie walked up with a conspiratorial grin. "Those were my idea. Aren't they delicious?"

"Mm–hmph." Kate finally swallowed. "Good choice. Now that I've had the dessert, I better get to the main course."

Ham, turkey, and shrimp filled one end of the next table. Tom knew how to throw a party! She filled a plate, committing to running a few extra miles tomorrow.

Festive holiday music played, and the party pulsated with lively conversations among staff, their families, and some of Davis Printing's key customers. This was not your typical hollow, pro-forma party. It was a genuine celebration. People were looking ahead. The company's plans were exciting, and they had already produced re- sults. Repeat business had increased. Niche specialties, customization, and design had attracted both small and large firms.

Kate considered the changes in the past year: a new large-format digital press, cross functional collabora- tion, new markets, and reliance on situational analysis. The Situational Mindsets process established a common language that respected different points of view. And a sustained rhythm of high productivity and congeniali- ty had replaced the former nonstop, all–hands–on–deck, emergency–in–progress atmosphere. The place hummed.

Situational Mindsets had also reeled in a few whales. They were the biggest companies the firm had ever served. They had a great deal to celebrate.

"Excuse me, Kate." Richard had come up on her right. "You know my beautiful wife, Jess."

"Of course. How are you? You look great."

"Fine, thanks. I'm getting out more now that the baby is a month old." Jess smiled, then tilted her head slightly. "It's a great party, isn't it?"

"Is it *always* this extravagant?" Kate asked.

"Tom's outdone himself this year. And he shows more excitement than ever." Jess nodded toward him laughing with a group near the dessert table.

Kate looked around at the smiling, engaged crowd. "It's been a great year." A new spirit permeated the firm. Planning and trust had translated into growth and employee satisfaction. "I haven't had a chance to speak to Tom yet. He's been so busy schmoozing with everyone."

"He's over there admiring the cake." Richard looked past Kate. "Let me go and say hi. I'll catch up with you later."

Tom's voice carried over the crowd as he spoke with Alice Notley. "In some ways, it's the same company I started up decades ago. We're dedicated to customer service. So, we've expanded to provide a full menu of services. I thought the good old days were great. But what we're doing now beats those days by a mile."

Richard broke in to say hello and moved on.

As Kate joined Tom and Alice, he smiled broadly and looked at her. "I hope you're enjoying yourself."

"It's quite the event," she said.

"Best day of the year."

Alice spotted a friend and excused herself.

Tom continued softly. "I have a surprise announcement to make tonight."

Kate was stunned.

"Did you notice Hal Brigham over there?"

Kate's eyes widened. "From Print Right?"

"He's retiring soon. Davis is buying his firm."

"*Whoa!* You're planning an acquisition?"

"We've known each other for years, and he thinks it's the right time for him to retire. Said he's only comfortable selling his business to Davis. He knows we offer quality work and stand behind it. We operate much as they do, so it should be a reasonably smooth integration. And he'll help transfer his former customers to us."

"That's great."

"Sure, and we'll keep most of his staff too. There are a few who'll be retiring, though. This growth will open up promotions for our staff."

"I had no idea ..."

"We've lots to celebrate, Kate. But let me make a few announcements and acknowledge the folks who made this an outstanding year." He walked to the center of the room.

"Everyone"—he lifted his hand above his head—"can I have your attention, please. I want to recognize our outstanding employees, not only with praise but also with a tangible thank you. When I call your name, please come forward for the recognition you deserve—along with a bonus check. Then we can continue to celebrate what we've accomplished. Happy Holidays and Happy New Year to you all!"

P A R T

TWO

Situational Mindset Agility

11

Applying the Situational Mindsets Model

"When you talk, you are only repeating what you already know. But if you listen, you may learn something new."

— *HH The 14th Dalai Lama*

In Part One, Kate Hollander joined Davis Printing and immediately recognized the need for change—but not just in Sales. Certainly, the Sales Department was not meeting its quota, but in addition, customers were complaining, turfdoms flourished, and the owner operated with a crisis mentality. His practice was to try to plug every hole rather than step back and tackle larger issues.

Kate took time to study the systems, meet the people, recognize their concerns, and recommend viable alternatives. For Sales, she instituted radical change, while for the organization she proposed evolutionary adjustments. Applying Situational Mindsets, she was able to distinguish what was needed and how to muster support for an initiative.

Part Two presents an in-depth examination of the practice of Situational Mindsets. It answers the questions of *exactly* what Situational Mindsets is and what benefits it provides practitioners.

Definition and Uses

A Situational Mindset is a:

- Filter, lens, or frame of reference for collecting and evaluating information

- Comprehensive scan of current conditions

- Point of view about what is critical at this juncture

The use of Situational Mindsets benefits those who are:

- Refining goals and plans based on new realities

- Brainstorming ideas and generating alternatives

- Evaluating options

- Weighing potential risks and consequences

- Seeking to gain support for implementation

- Persuading others to engage or commit

Evaluating Situations

Similar to Kate's medical triage process, using Situational Mindsets depends on gathering current information. Medics collect relevant facts—respiration, vital signs, mental stability, and so on—to decide what action to take. A practice we all should follow since we regularly confront tough choices and have limited resources and time. We must decide what takes precedence and focus on achieving that goal.

When conditions shift, when complexity increases, when information is ambiguous, or when we tackle precedent-setting decisions, we must consider all six Situational Mindsets in order to decide which takes priority based on current conditions. These Situational Mindsets include the:

- **Inventing Mindset:** A priority addressing innovation, creativity, leveraged technology, breakthrough ideas, and organizational synergies

- **Catalyzing Mindset:** An emphasis on customer service, retention, competitive position, fast action, and market growth

- **Developing Mindset:** An internal focus on accountabilities, infrastructure, systems, standards, budget allocations, policies, and strategy

- **Performing Mindset:** A priority on quality, ROI, workflow, efficiency, productivity, process monitoring, and project management

- **Protecting Mindset:** A focus on teamwork, culture, talent, turnover, engagement, trust, and succession planning

- **Challenging Mindset:** A concentration on validating assumptions, monitoring trends, identifying risks, preparing for the future, analyzing new business models, and scouting for alliances

All of these Mindsets add valuable insights to successfully navigate change. Using them requires mental agility and refusal to hunker down and hope it will pass us by. It won't. If anything, it will hit us when we are not looking. The best priority, however, depends on the situation.

Choosing a Mindset

We may be tempted to think we can juggle all six Mindsets equally. In actuality, multitasking merely produces confusion, uncertainty, delay, and mistakes. For example, some leaders direct their staffs to operate faster, cheaper, better—an unattainable mandate. A manufacturer might improve a product, but it will probably not be cheaper or faster. Neither will reducing cost typically translate into a higher-quality product. Choices must be made. We cannot accomplish all three of these criteria at once, nor can we meet goals in all six Mindsets at once.

When one priority is achieved, a new one rises to the top. A leader might focus on increasing market share by 5 percent, but after that is realized, the priority may shift to expanding facilities to handle the increase in business. After increasing capacity, yet another priority might surface focusing on improving quality. Even after we select a priority, we must continually check for changes and adjust as conditions warrant.

Hockey great Wayne Gretzky famously explained that he always skated to where the puck would be rather than where it had been.[1] Like hockey pucks, Mindset priorities move. We need to focus on where they are and consider where they might be heading.

Determining Others' Mindsets

Besides providing a method for approaching change, Situational Mindsets also offers a path to objective and respectful discussions. Instead of guessing, inferring, or judging based on subjective factors, Mindsets relies on questions to learn what is driving another person. Open-ended questions such as "What is your goal?" or "What is the top priority?" easily reveal another's desired outcomes. A less formal query like "What is keeping you awake at night?" also discloses what is top of mind.

We can also detect Mindset priorities through observation. What action is a person taking? What metrics matter the most? To which department is the company allocating additional resources? Is the client shifting resources to support customer growth rather than new equipment? Are they hiring staff for quality improvement efforts rather than research? Each observation provides a clue to the prevailing Mindset.

Handling Change

Tom's decision to hire Kate proved an extremely smart move. Not only did she understand sales, but she also knew how to handle complexity and change. And it started with understanding the lay of the land within Davis Printing. She studied and swiftly grasped fluid circumstances, identified system interactions, and discovered productive solutions. She knew that change creates stress and elicits defensiveness. What one person sees as an undeniable opportunity, another perceives as an ominous threat. She recognized the need to go slow at first to enlist others so she could achieve faster progress down the road.

People rarely greet new things with unabashed enthusiasm—unless it is a pay increase. This makes effective change management one of the most sought-after talents but one that is rare. Aligning support requires questioning, listening, understanding, and adjusting. We must see and appreciate the viewpoints of others. As leaders, instead of pushing change by autocratic fiat, we have to expand our perceptions and situational awareness. This means accepting that we function with a limited perspective.

Consider the following question: How many squares are in the drawing below?

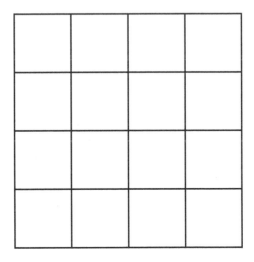

Most people answer sixteen or seventeen. That is correct since *every* single box, as well as the whole illustration, is squares. Yet groupings of four single boxes also constitute squares. We just do not *see* all thirty squares at first glance. More than 90 percent of respondents are content with identifying sixteen or seventeen.

This highlights an important reality: when we find *an* answer, any answer, we typically stop searching. Of course, this illustration is very simple, making it easy to jump to a conclusion. In business, very little is simple, and gaining agreement from a diverse group is challenging. We need to stop accepting things and start studying complex issues from all perspectives. Instead of thinking we know everything, we have to dig deeper and broader to gain a complete picture. The practice of Situational Mindsets offers insights, solutions, and *aha* moments, even if a situation initially appears familiar or obvious.

The past seduces us. What worked last year appears safe, but it is not guaranteed to be successful. Guarantees expire. This truth is at least as old as Ecclesiastes 3:1, "To every thing there is a season, and a time to every purpose under the heaven" (KJV). Our job is to identify what will no longer work, what will work now, and what alternatives exist for us in the short and long term. Examining current conditions helps us let go of outworn viewpoints, assumptions, and practices.

Situational Mindsets provides a roadmap to fully understand the situation, identify emerging options, and prevent impulsive acts. Seeing beneath surface indicators and recognizing patterns enable us to seize opportunities, avoid pitfalls, and detect possibilities.

When complexity and ambiguity prevail or when it is essential to get something right the first time, we have to analyze risks and consider ramifications. We cannot skip over minor elements or details but need to understand the entire picture before leaping into action. The ready-

fire-aim practice curtails analysis and can threaten the survival of an organization as well as careers.

Smart choices stem from the disciplined approach of 'ready, *aim*, fire.' The question is how we can make sure our 'aim' is true. We cannot rely on old data, past practices, or wishful thinking; however, Situational Mindsets ensures a comprehensive understanding of current conditions, opportunities, and risks. It requires a commitment to use all six Mindset lenses to collect information, evaluate alternatives, and select the best route, given current realities. Fortunately, Situational Mindsets is a practice everyone can easily master.

Going Slow or Fast?

Acting on gut feelings or intuition can work in a stable environment. Instinct and intuition are aspects of our evolutionary survival equipment. However, research shows that knee-jerk responses betray us as we confront complex situations.

A little experiment. Quickly answer the following question: How many animals of each species did Moses take on his ark? Most people instantly respond with *two* and are confident in their answer. But if they had carefully analyzed the entire question before replying, most would have answered differently. Actually, it was Noah, not Moses, who built the ark, so *Moses* did not take any animals onto the ark.

This automatic response does not stem from faulty knowledge of the Old Testament but from concentrating narrowly on the first part of the question without examining the full context. The last section was assumed and, therefore, went unexamined.

Accident- and crime-scene witness statements frequently illustrate our tendency to observe and register what we think is important while overlooking other aspects. Hit-and-run accident witnesses disagree on the color or make of the car involved. Similarly, selective vision prevails in criminal cases. Information from the Innocence Project, which investigates cases of suspected wrongful conviction, reveals that witness misidentification was involved in 70 percent of 358 wrongful convictions that were exonerated using DNA evidence.[2]

Quick conclusions, cursory reviews, and gut responses offer a fast response, and we may think our job is done. We saw what we saw. The trouble is that acting on our first impressions stops us from collecting sufficient evidence or confirming our assumptions. These failures are due to:

- Concentrating on confirming data while ignoring information to the contrary

- Collecting information only from one function, specialization, or territory

- Trying to simultaneously collect data and evaluate information

- Valuing speed over accuracy

When faced with change, uncertainty, and complexity, we must collect and weigh all key data from all points of view.

At Davis Printing, Tom pressured Kate to hit the ground running. His focus on quick action shortchanged the need to unravel systemic internal tensions, analyze customer requirements, and balance short- and long-term goals. Kate's choice to "go slow in order to go fast" allowed her to identify and address specific problems, find gaps, and propose new practices. None of which could have happened had she merely exhorted her staff push harder. Working smarter always trumps working harder.

Knowing Your Environment

In the face of change, sticking with the status quo is reckless. Our dynamic environment presents new opportunities and unforeseen risks, making situational awareness vital. Ignoring our environment is analogous to discounting Mother Nature. It invites trouble.

In the 1990s, mortgage companies expected home prices to continue climbing. They offered subprime mortgages, assuming buyers could use their equity to refinance later.[3] They paid a high price for relying on the past. In little more than a decade, the housing market collapsed, revealing their error. More recently, grocery chains assumed there would never be serious online competition. Energy companies misjudged the demand for oil and price points.

Change regularly rocks industries. The healthcare alliance formed by Berkshire Hathaway, JP Morgan Chase, and Amazon suddenly shifted health-industry assumptions. Setting anything in stone today is arrogant, ignorant, and dangerous. Only continuous, real-time adjustment delivers sustained success. Some firms have paid dearly for ignoring or miscalculating their present realities.

Most of us are not responsible for formulating the strategic direction for an international firm, but blunders occur at all levels. Everyone has to know what is real, what is emerging, and what is required to achieve outstanding results.

One company came to me after they launched an updated product. Their enthusiasm had obscured the need to prepare call-center scripts describing the new offering. The oversight spoiled the launch by confusing both staff and customers calling for information. They corrected the error, and the company eventually recovered but getting it right the first time would have been smarter, less stressful, and less expensive. In this case, a small executive group had planned and implemented the change with a need-to-know approach. They had failed to confer with key players and missed an important execution step. Had they invested the time to explore current realities, they could have dodged the ding to their reputation. Instead, their compartmentalization masked critical aspects and created confusion. Everyone needs to understand key elements, how they contribute, and how success will be measured.

When the story in this book opened, Kate took time to evaluate the situation at Davis Printing. Tom used micromanagement, tolerated silos, and accepted the persistent tension between Sales and Production as inevitable. Sticking to outdated sales practices, accepting poor internal alignment, and adopting a nose-to-the-grindstone mentality hurt the business.

Kate uprooted his acceptance of the status quo. She promoted Situational Mindsets and consultative selling, implemented new systems, rejected hasty conclusions, and encouraged information sharing and cooperation. Informed by Situational Mindsets analysis, she engaged the key players, surfaced more information, and closed blind spots. They also encouraged Tom to switch his management practice and focus on future growth.

Choosing Collaboration

Hierarchical command-and-control and other aspects of authoritarianism stifle the information exchange, innovation, initiative, and commitment that are essential to success. Authoritarianism and the need-to-know mentality worked in the early industrial age, but they are destructive in the digital age. Command-and-control limits job satisfaction, opportunity, and creativity.

Tom's micromanagement gave him the illusion that he was in control, but he and his employees were floundering. Situational Mindsets and its focus on objective data and analysis improved collaboration, growth, and bottom line.

Successful leaders know the value of analyzing, sharing, and engaging. The supreme allied commander in Europe during World War II, General Dwight D. Eisenhower, wielded immense power and could have adopted a command-and-control style. Instead, he wisely chose to engage, communicate, listen, and influence others to win active support.[4] "You do not lead by hitting people over the head," he said. "That's assault, not leadership."[5]

The question for us today is whether we value collaboration over confusion and false steps. We have the opportunity to seek firsthand input from employees and stir respectful, unfiltered debate. Although it is tempting to pursue every avenue and opportunity, we must make choices based on realities and then target critical priorities.

Identifying Your Current Mindset

Choosing your priority Situational Mindset enables you to share your thinking with others, establish plans, and clarify expectations. Your priority determines what you buy, what you decide, and what you resist.

Consider how mindsets impact the decision to buy a car. A buyer with a safety-first mindset prefers a high safety rating, while another person might choose to buy a car with the newest technology and styling. And a third might elect fuel economy, resale value, seating capacity, price, or insurance costs as the most critical factor in decision-making.

As a buyer, you set your particular requirements given your current context, and you must make trade-offs to achieve those prerequisites. For example, you may establish the top price you are willing to pay, only to discover that for a few hundred dollars more, a different model delivers better mileage and higher resale value. Collecting information and balancing options will establish what is the best choice.

The following sample questions from my Situational Mindsets Indicator provide a snapshot of your present Mindset for one specific task. Before answering these questions, identify a current challenging work situation, task, project, or assignment. Then, for each question, circle the most important option at this time for your situation. Every alternative presents a solid choice for your situation, so there are no wrong answers.

Questions:

1. In this situation, an effective leader should first:

   A. Search for innovative solutions
   B. Stress the need for customer service and action
   C. Develop a work plan and set accountability and performance standards
   D. Stress the importance of continuous improvement
   E. Engage key players and encourage teamwork
   F. Scan emerging opportunities and threats

2. You face a difficult decision. What will you do first?

   A. Generate multiple potential solutions
   B. Consider how the decision will impact customers and sales
   C. Develop a system to analyze alternatives and impact
   D. Calculate a cost–benefit analysis
   E. Collect information from others and engage them in the decision-making process
   F. Question the assumption associated with the situation

3. How would an organization that has successfully handled this type of situation in the past be described?

   A. Innovative
   B. Customer focused and market driven
   C. Well organized with seamless execution
   D. Efficient with high-quality products/services
   E. Collaborative culture with a talented workforce
   F. Strategically driven

Scoring:

Count the number of times you circled each letter. If all of your selections were the same letter, you currently operate from a single Mindset. If you have circled more than one letter, you are using multiple Mindsets.

Selected Letter	Mindset Priority
A	Inventing
B	Catalyzing
C	Developing
D	Performing
E	Protecting
F	Challenging

Now that you have identified your Mindset for one situation, it is time to examine each Mindset. The next chapter describes the Situational Mindsets and sample questions to check that you have fully examined each one. The practice of Situational Mindsets increases your ability to face escalating uncertainty and complexity.

12

Mastering the Mindsets

"If one does not know to which port one is sailing, no wind is favorable."

— *Lucius Annaeus Seneca*

Situational Mindsets analysis begins by determining what is vital *at this time* within our external and internal realities. External factors such as changes in regulations, technology, economic conditions, customer requirements, and competition must be balanced with internal aspects such as staffing and workload, engagement and culture, resources, facilities, and systems.

After assessing our realities, we can determine our current priorities. Just as our needs determine whether to use PowerPoint or Excel, we choose a different Mindset priority based on pressing issues. Neither software nor Mindsets are set in stone, what is best depends on current circumstances.

The following sections identify each Situational Mindset's benefits and areas of concentration. Using these terms facilitates communication by providing a vocabulary everyone understands. The Mindsets also spur critical thinking and prevent blinding tunnel vision. Using Mindsets avoids subjective distractions such as personal intentions and stereotypes.

Inventing Mindset

"To cease to think creatively is to cease to live."
— *Benjamin Franklin*

The Inventing Mindset targets innovative products, services, methodologies, and synergies. It values leveraging technology and introducing new processes and practices. Encouraging breakthrough thinking, this Mindset promotes developing state-of-the-art products and services.

Steve Jobs said, "Let's go invent tomorrow rather than worrying about what happened yesterday."[1] Certainly, when he ran Pixar Animation Studios or launched the iPod, iPhone, and iPad, he displayed inventiveness and strong support for an innovative culture. But anyone can adopt and encourage out-of-the-box thinking. Genius is not required. The ability to promote fresh ideas, explore unconventional solutions, surmount barriers, design new products, revise systems, and adopt novel approaches stems from a priority to innovate.

No organization can thrive if it squashes original thinking. Nor can it remain viable if it is a me-too organization, merely duplicating another's business model or products.

Davis Printing
At Davis Printing, Kate employed the Inventing Mindset to introduce the Situational Mindsets framework and spur creative customer-based solutions. She instituted consultative sales to improve revenue and created synergies with Production. The Inventing Mindset also drove her recommendations for new product lines such as product

labels, specialty conference products, and signage. Several of her efforts at Davis demonstrated an Inventing Mindset.

Focal Points

The distinctive focal points of the Inventing Mindset are:

- Embracing new ideas and technology

- Encouraging creative thinking

- Improving products and services

- Promoting creativity in others

- Removing organizational barriers by using technology

- Leveraging cross-functional knowledge

- Developing creative alternatives

- Applying solutions to increase effectiveness and improve the brand

Guiding Questions

To stimulate the Inventing Mindset, reflect on the following questions:

Creative-Thinking Questions

- *What will outside-the-box thinking reveal?*
  - This discussion not only spurs creative thinking but also uncovers innovative alternatives.

- *What could we do if there were absolutely no constraints?*
  - Removing existing restrictions releases different ways to approach processes, resource utilization, and operating practices.

- *What would we discover if we sought the opposite result?*

  — Considering contrary goals can release productivity, uncover existing impediments, expose outworn assumptions, and reveal potential. This question demonstrates a willingness to expand viewpoints and challenge accepted practices.

- *What have we never tried?*

  — This question stimulates creative alternatives and ways of working together. Certainly, it encourages thinking beyond traditionally safe responses.

- *Have we spent sufficient time brainstorming?*

  — Too often, teams move directly from data collection into the solution-finding phase without considering the entire range of options. Allocating time to identify possibilities before acting broadens the scope of alternatives. People also tend to accept a good idea without an effective search for the best idea.

- *What is the ideal product or service?*

  — This question generates alternatives—moving beyond an existing customer base, leveraging technology, tapping into existing talents. When we are free to envision the possibilities, dramatic improvements follow.

Unconventional Analysis Questions

- *What alternatives or new approaches are there?*

  — Everyone has ideas about opportunities, processes, or practices, but most fail to voice them. Asking this question signals interest and supports new thoughts.

- *What new combinations or synergies are possible?*

  — Innovation often arises from the cross-fertilization of ideas across disciplines, functions, and units. Modifying processes can simplify practices, streamline communication, identify gaps, curtail redundancies, and monitor progress. This question surfaces fresh ways of doing things.

- *What was rejected or failed in the past—might it be viable now?*

  — Innovation can be stymied by the it-will-never-work-here or the already-tried-that assumption. Times and circumstances change, and something that was infeasible in the past may be entirely viable today.

Never underestimate the power of questions. Thomas Edison benefited from his inexhaustible urge to ask questions and explore other avenues. While working on the incandescent electric lamp, he tested ten thousand materials in his search for the best filament.[2] We need to keep asking ourselves what we can do better.

Edison was not only an inveterate questioner and creative thinker, but he was intent on selling his inventive products, a Mindset not shared by all researchers. For example, Xerox PARC—today known as PARC (Palo Alto Research Center Incorporated)—earned a legendary reputation as a highly productive R&D lab. Their work on the graphical user interface (GUI) revolutionized computing, but Xerox PARC did not bring it to market. They failed to commercialize GUI and their other discoveries. Patents and breakthrough products are marvelous, but without customers, the investment in R&D is wasteful. To reap the rewards of innovation, the Inventing Mindset must pivot to the Catalyzing Mindset and offer its advancements to customers.

Catalyzing Mindset

"The customer is always right."
— Unknown

The Catalyzing Mindset targets the marketplace, selling products/services, providing customer service, and growing the customer base while retaining key customers. This Mindset responds rapidly to user feedback and changing customer requirements to build a competitive edge. It closely monitors competitors in order to surpass them, and it uncompromisingly takes advantage of market opportunities.

Zeroing in on shifting competition, the Catalyzing Mindset's critical yardsticks include growing market share and territory, increasing sales volume, surpassing the competition, and seizing hot trends. Examples of customer-centric responses to market change include:

- Personalized service at Nordstrom combined with e-commerce

- Free shipping and media-channel access from Amazon Prime

- Banking cafés from Capital One

- Price-match guarantee at Best Buy

- Renting designer clothes at Rent the Runway

From the Catalyzing Mindset point of view, the customer is king, queen, and star rolled into one. This Mindset optimistically assumes that dedicated, focused efforts move mountains, surmount barriers, and guarantee customer loyalty. Nike's slogan, 'Just Do It,' reflects this commitment to fast action, as does Captain Picard's "Make it so" on the *USS Enterprise-D* in *Star Trek: The Next Generation*. Driven by a strong desire to get things done, the Catalyzing Mindset finds practical solutions and remains dedicated to improving sales growth and dominating the market.

Davis Printing

Tom Davis's singular mandate that Kate swiftly boost sales reflects a Catalyzing Mindset. His hastiness was imprudent; however, fast action can be wise. US Navy rear admiral and computer scientist Grace Hopper voiced this spirit when she quoted the old saying, "It's much easier to apologize than to get permission."[3] The Catalyzing Mindset adopts the act-first-and-deal-with-repercussions-later philosophy. However, this approach can also be reckless since it may rely on deploying standard practices rather than investigating alternatives.

Kate exercised the Catalyzing Mindset when she sought consultative sales and B2B opportunities, highlighted design services, and worked toward establishing Davis Printing as a one-stop printer. In addition to wanting to expand the firm's reach and lock in customers, she worked with Brian Lewis to keep a sale and retain a customer.

Just as a platoon lieutenant orders the unit to "take that hill," the Catalyzing Mindset operates with clear goals and desired outcomes in the hope that they will not only be met but exceeded. This Mindset displays initiative and energy to achieve results and stay on top of the market.

Focal Points

The Catalyzing Mindset priority concentrates on:

- Gaining new customers

- Collecting customer feedback

- Beating the competition

- Retaining key customers

- Meeting or exceeding sales goals

- Responding quickly to opportunities

- Building customer loyalty

- Closing profitable contracts

- Offering strong customer service

The Catalyzing Mindset priority surfaces when there is a new product launch, when new customer segments emerge, when customer requirements shift, or when competitors threaten a company's brand.

Whether serving internal or external customers, the Catalyzing Mindset boldly defines success by using customer-based metrics and meeting sales quotas. It is noted for aggressive initiatives and promoting action. A BHAG (big hairy audacious goal) captures this priority's can-do approach. This Mindset guards against complacency, mediocrity, excessive caution, and burdensome constraints to retain a strong customer focus.

Guiding Questions

The following questions develop the Catalyzing Mindset:

Customer-Centric Questions

- *Who are our key customers?*

— While this seems like an obvious question, it is not always an easy question to answer. A company may have some customers who place large orders and others who deliver large profits. Which group is key?

- *What will gain and retain our key customers?*

  — One customer group may find value in innovation (Apple), while another prizes lower prices (Wal-Mart). Firms that fail to closely connect with their customers invite disruption. Each audience segment must be closely monitored.

- *How can we expand our customer base?*

  — Markets are not stagnant, so staying up-to-date is critical. Even advertising has to align with the intended customer. Should the ad be in print or on social media? In addition to catering to existing customers, organizations need to reach out to potential customers.

Market Questions

- *Who/what is the competition?*

  — Competitors pop up unexpectedly. The Catalyzing Mindset studies up-and-coming contenders as well as traditional rivals for potential challenges to market position.

- *What will keep us ahead of the competition?*

  — The answer is always a moving target. Perhaps it is faster customer service, better features, rightsizing products and services, loyalty reward programs, extended offerings, faster delivery, bulk pricing, awards, or higher-quality products. Whatever it is, a company that outpaces the competition will thrive.

- *What are additional market options?*
  - The do-it-now aspect of the Catalyzing Mindset must be balanced against constant awareness of potential markets. Alternative options might include moving up or down the value chain, changing the geographical scope, altering delivery channels or schedules, adopting different service or quality standards, or identifying new alliances to guarantee continued success.

Operations Questions

- *What will meet our schedule?*
  - Getting things out the door on time builds customer loyalty. However, schedules must be realistic. Knowing what it takes to deliver on time prevents overpromising and underdelivering, which strain customer loyalty.

- *What will enhance customer service?*
  - Initiative and discretionary effort stem from clear objectives, supportive systems, effective rewards, and timely multi-channel communication. Customer feedback, visits, and current knowledge foster a customer-first mentality throughout the organization.

- *Whose support do we need?*
  - Too often this question centers on who can authorize or finance a project. In fact, implementers remain critical to making things happen. Working to gain and sustain support from all players pays dividends. If a problem emerges, supporters can be counted on to quickly pitch in and resolve the issue.

The Catalyzing Mindset priority concentrates on custom-ers, branding, sales, competitive position, and market growth. Since customers continually ask, "What can you do for me today?" attention to their needs and market trends must be relentless.

But without effective execution, companies cannot continue to retain customers or brand. They have to ful-fill their promises through outstanding customer service. This requires sound internal systems, clear policies, and sufficient capacity—a shift to the Developing Mindset.

Developing Mindset

"If you build castles in the air, your work need not be lost; that is where they should be. Now put the foundations under them."
— *Henry David Thoreau*

The Developing Mindset prioritizes a robust infrastructure, sound policies to guide action, clear accountabilities, strategic goals, and integrated systems for internal excellence.

Consistent, effective, and resilient systems do not happen by accident. They result from incessant orchestration, planning, capacity building, infrastructure, and smart allocation of resources. One and done is never the case. Relying on a single design, system, or structure invites dysfunction. The perfect organization remains elusive. Management icon W. Edwards Deming found that 85 percent of an organization's problems lay with its systems, processes, structures, and management practices, whereas only 15 percent could be attributed to middle and frontline employees.[4]

This Mindset focuses intensely on governance, systems, and coordination to avoid silos, gaps, and suboptimization. Since every organization is perfectly designed to get the results it is currently getting, improvement requires adjustments. The problem is that most organizations expect better results without changing systems, policies, or structures. They fail to realize that issues such as pay levels, reporting relationships, span of control, levels of autonomy, and accountabilities impact goal achievement. Every organization must consider its industry, mission, tradition, strategy, business model, and culture. A follow-the-leader organizational design cannot deliver seamless operations.

Investment in planning paves the road to success. Designing information flow, determining the chain of command, and establishing accountabilities reduce confusion and promotes long-term viability and excellence.

Davis Printing

At Davis Printing, Kate used the Developing Mindset when she created the customer-service team, combining insights from Debbie, Joann, and Ron. This cross-functional team was perfectly positioned to review and resolve customer concerns. Richard, also, exhibited the Developing Mindset when he requested additional staffing and equipment to cope with the increased demand.

Although the Developing Mindset establishes systems and structures, these should not become burdensome or fixed. Minimal structure encourages agility and change readiness. Excessive structure breeds bureaucracy.

Focal Points

The Developing Mindset adds value by:

- Identifying goals and allocating resources

- Setting clear expectations and norms

- Balancing autonomy and oversight

- Establishing clear levels of accountability

- Designing seamless systems

- Creating policy to guide performance

- Forming multiple information channels

- Creating effective monitoring systems

- Aligning team responsibilities, tasks, and resources

This Mindset must function throughout the organization. Mid-level leaders need to organize work, provide clear guidance, delegate effectively, and implement best practices. Their attention to crafting job descriptions, setting performance goals, and clarifying reporting relationships ensures performance and sustains excellence.

Guiding Questions

Key questions for the Developing Mindset target three areas:

Systems Questions

- *What do we expect of ourselves? What is the plan?*
  - Goals, milestones, and metrics align actions and monitor progress. Attention to these questions avoids confusion and reduces risk.

- *What is the best structure for us?*
  - Optimal organizational design promotes—but does not guarantee—high performance levels, effective communication, seamless coordination, and clear guidance.

- *What systems will deliver effective coordination and goal achievement?*
  - Integrated systems simplify monitoring, speed action, provide timely information, and promote cross-functional collaboration.

- *How can technology improve operations?*
  - Technology heightens efficiencies, supports collaboration, and increases on-time performance.

- *How should information flow?*

  — Relying solely on vertical communication delays and distorts information. Lateral communication and functional networks improve productivity, spark critical thinking, and foster seamless operations.

Policy Questions

- *What is the optimal balance between autonomy and control?*

  — An appropriate balance between delegating to the lowest level possible and providing sufficient oversight and control encourages accountability, engagement, initiative, and performance.

- *What policies will ensure success?*

  — Policies can become outdated and stifling or insufficient and confusing. Melding centralized standards with unit and individual initiatives can be tricky. Accepting disparity creates silos, risk, and low levels of commitment.

- *How will we manage conflict?*

  — Focusing on Mindsets and objective data keeps the conversation open, respectful, and productive. Conflicts rarely develop when goals, expectations, and resolution paths are clear.

Execution Questions

- *How can we guarantee sustained, outstanding results?*

  — Excellence requires effective planning, seamless operations, appropriate resource allocation, and adjustment to changing realities. Well-monitored, comprehensive metrics identify deficiencies and dysfunction before they impact productivity or derail goals.

- *How will we measure results?*

  — Measured activities merit attention and effort, so they are typically fulfilled. However, measurements have to be comprehensive, or they will distort behavior. Non-quantified measurements such as innovation, collaboration, system effectiveness, and a high-performing culture must be included on any scorecard.

- *What level of teaming and collaboration is necessary?*

  — Teams consistently outperform individual efforts but only when a team's structure matches its task, and the team has an appropriate level of authority. Defining the type of team and the type of collaboration produces engagement, trust, creative thinking, and productivity.

- *What is the appropriate level of risk?*

  — Avoiding all risk may appear prudent, but companies that are highly risk averse miss opportunities and become stagnant. The acceptable level of risk depends on the industry, the organization's life-cycle stage, and external realities such as changes to the competitive landscape or shifts in the global economy.

- *How do we reinforce achievement?*

  — We must acknowledge, celebrate, and reward accomplishments at individual, team, unit, and organizational levels. If we do not recognize achievement, mediocrity blossoms.

- *Do we employ problem-solving teams or task forces to handle complex problems?*

  — Complex issues necessitate cross-functional expertise, experience, and perspective. When the right people work together, perceptive questions emerge, and brilliant ideas follow.

After we have established effective systems, structures, and policies, priorities typically shift to fine-tuning procedures, streamlining workflow, reducing costs, managing vendors, enhancing quality, and maximizing financial return. These are the dominant interests of the Performing Mindset.

Performing Mindset

"The best thought-out plans in the world aren't worth the paper they're written on if you can't pull them off."

— **Ralph S. Larsen,** *Chairman and CEO, Johnson & Johnson, 1989–2002*

The Performing Mindset concentrates on streamlining work processes for maximum efficiency, productivity, and profit. Interest centers on improving quality and production-cycle time, establishing an effective supply chain, controlling inventory, reducing waste, and boosting the bottom line.

To accomplish this, the Performing Mindset relies on data and would not operate without it any more than you would drive your car blindfolded. This frame of reference prizes quantifiable and qualitative measures over instinct. However, the Mindset goes beyond the green-eyeshade stereotype to a ready-aim-fire approach that translates data into meaningful information and results.

It calibrates existing practices, then vigilantly tracks performance to update metrics and establish best practices. Data analysis uncovers patterns, gaps, obstructions, and deviations, which signal the need for action.

Armed with this intelligence, the Performing Mindset seeks to correct and prevent problems. Its goals are to remove unproductive activities, leverage technological solutions, and improve quality, efficiency, and productivity.

Davis Printing

Tom Davis's concentration on cash flow and reluctance to assume a potentially burdensome debt reflect the Performing Mindset's attention to the bottom line. Naturally, his staff recognized his priority and presented ideas to him based on that. To minimize the cost until quantifiable benefits could be verified, Kate requested a CRM pilot program, enabling Tom to assess the actual value through a quarterly rather than an annual software subscription. Richard proposed outsourcing to trade shops rather than immediately pressing Tom to purchase a press. This reflected his awareness of Tom's close attention to the bottom line and his cautious approach to assuming risk.

Ensuring quality, establishing a reliable workflow, and improving cycle time and financial health are hallmarks of the Performing Mindset.

Focal Points

The values of this Mindset include:

- Using data to detect patterns and deviations
- Monitoring and measuring progress for just-in-time corrections
- Setting individual and unit performance standards
- Adjusting resources at critical junctures
- Improving workflow and procedures
- Enhancing quality
- Increasing safety
- Standardizing operating practices
- Reducing waste and warranty costs

- Improving cycle time

- Managing the supply chain

- Increasing financial return and the bottom line

Guiding Questions

Preventing problems and improving work procedures flow from the Performing Mindset's attention to the following questions:

Measurement Questions

- *Do our measures cover all six Mindsets?*

  — Using a wider range of indicators increases efficiency and outstanding performance. After all, what gets measured gets done. A balanced set of metrics covers all relevant factors to avoid skewed performance.

- *Are practices and expectations tailored to local conditions?*

  — A one-size-fits-all approach never works for long. Customized measures deliver exceptional results. And those measures can be used to set realistic expectations and reward excellence.

- *Are we using both lagging and leading indicators?*

  — Lagging, or after-the-fact, assessment reveals what is past, and the results are already locked in. Leading, or in-process, metrics capture current realities, enabling significant just-in-time opportunities to tweak practices and improve results.

- *Is information from customers, suppliers, employees, stakeholders, regulators, and performance metrics captured and used?*

— We must know how we are doing from multiple perspectives before we finalize goals, plans, and decisions. Limiting the scope of data collection is like wearing blinders.

- *Do we measure both quantitative and qualitative aspects?*

  — Hard, quantitative information presents only part of the picture. Qualitative measures offer a distinct point of view that must be calibrated. Peter Drucker famously said, "Culture eats strategy for breakfast."[5] We must pay attention to the soft stuff.

Execution Questions

- *Do our systems provide insightful overviews as well as needed detail at all levels?*

  — Relevant information at a macro as well as a microlevel must be customized and shared to all levels of the organization.

- *Do we employ modeling, simulations, pilot tests, and experimentation appropriately?*

  — Bet-the-ranch decisions are dangerous and unnecessary, particularly when pilots can reveal risks and guide implementation.

- *Is everyone committed to continuous improvement?*

  — Sponsors, analysts, and implementers must all vigorously support continuous improvement. Otherwise, poor systems or processes drown quality and efficiency.

- *Do we adjust resources to ensure critical deliverables?*

  — Nothing is more frustrating than an exciting initiative falling short due to underfunding or limited resources.

- *Do we allocate resources for maximum effectiveness?*
  - — Maximum effectiveness differs from maximum efficiency. Short-term efficiency can short-circuit effectiveness by harming customer relations, sapping energy and innovation, increasing turnover, lowering morale, and diminishing productivity.

- *Are we monitoring performance across units, products, and processes?*
  - — Smoldering issues in one area can erupt into dangerous fires throughout an organization. Early warning alerts help to avoid major conflagrations.

Improvement Questions

- *Do we give timely feedback to cover issues within the person's control?*
  - — The most valuable feedback addresses actions within an individual's or team's control. Detailed insights add value and must replace general summaries.

- *Are we continually updating and communicating quality, project management, safety, and security practices?*
  - — Discovering ways to improve is only the first step toward actual improvement. Updated practices need to be communicated, accepted, and applied.

- *Are project-plan milestones sufficiently detailed to guide performance?*
  - — Grand ideas inspire, but only specific plans can be implemented.

- *Do we apply best-in-class standards?*
  - — Lip service to best-in-class practices cannot replace using them. Best practices have to be embedded, monitored, and recognized.

- *Do we use site visits to enhance high performance?*
  - — Site visits and staff exchanges explore new opportunities and practices.

- *Are targets realistic and challenging?*
  - — Stretch goals invigorate teams, provide personal growth, and ramp up energy. A fine line exists between challenging and unrealistic goals. Improbable goals demoralize.

Though the Performing Mindset targets efficiency and performance, it cannot sustain success by itself. Excessive protocols and cost-cutting imperil brand status, mental agility, and talent retention essential to long-term survivability. The loss of key employees is a costly blow. Lean and mean can become too lean and too mean without a balance from a Mindset focused on talent, teamwork, and culture. We must address such questions as "How can we protect our culture's DNA to maintain our competitive advantage?" and "Do we have the talent-bench strength and succession plans in place for long-term success?" These inquiries reflect the Protecting Mindset priority.

Protecting Mindset

"Opponents are working very hard to defeat us. Let's not do it for them by defeating ourselves from within."

— **John Wooden,** *Former UCLA Basketball Coach*

The Protecting Mindset spotlights employees, teamwork, and culture. Today's workforce expects a work environment that fosters autonomy, engagement, and developmental opportunities. Organizations offering career progression, respect, engagement, and transparency earn a reputation as a best place to work, which attracts and retains a talented workforce.

Supporting development, teamwork, and engagement sparks discretionary effort and initiative. The Protecting Mindset prioritizes a mission-driven culture, teamwork, high levels of collaboration, and effective succession planning. It advances esprit de corps, work-life balance, and employee satisfaction. Not that a high-performing culture can be achieved overnight.

Unlike electricity, culture cannot be turned on by a switch whenever needed. Believing that short-term attempts will significantly alter culture is delusional. Sustained attention is needed. A weak culture may appear benign, but it is like quicksand that will dangerously swamp an organization without warning. Culture creation requires a long, steady investment before it becomes institutionalized. But when it is embedded, it produces a competent, creative, collaborative, and dedicated workforce.

The Protecting Mindset ensures talented, vibrant employees. Not only does it foster pride and trust, but it also removes unnecessary distractions that stymie teamwork, information exchange, and collaboration. This Mindset strives to light a fire within employees as opposed to putting a fire under them. Smothering oversight and burdensome rules crush initiative and dedication. An open, respectful, and engaged workforce outperforms one beset by fear and micromanagement.

Davis Printing

At Davis Printing, Tom micromanaged due to his fear of being out of the loop. This devastating practice, which he thought would boost effectiveness, backfired by creating silos, hampering initiative, and reducing revenue. As a result, rumors, finger-pointing, and concealing bad news thrived. Moreover, focusing on daily details meant that he shirked his responsibility to prepare for the firm's future.

While Tom initially overlooked the importance of the Protecting Mindset, Kate's emphasis on teamwork, Richard's concentration on workforce planning, and Debbie's concerns over retention helped to raise his awareness and behavior. As his crisis thinking subsided, Tom recognized how talented his staff was and gave them the autonomy they deserved. At the year-end celebration, he handed out bonus checks in appreciation for them and their Protecting Mindsets.

Focal Points

Hallmarks of the Protecting Mindset include:

- Cultivating talent through training, coaching, and developmental opportunities

- Encouraging employee initiative and responsibility

- Establishing an environment that supports inquiry

- Building effective, integrated teams

- Recognizing the impact of respect and equitable practices on performance and retention

- Managing conflict objectively

- Implementing succession planning

- Constructing merit-based recognition and reward systems

- Building a best place to work

Although many of these actions are considered soft and difficult to measure, they contribute as much as the hard measures such as ROI and sales. Dealing with people combines science and art, meaning it is impossible to have a universal formula for all organizations. Culture requires constant tailoring, attention, and fine-tuning.

Focusing on development, initiative, involvement, recognition, and teamwork, this Mindset builds trust and confidence in the organization's fairness and transparency. An open exchange ensures continuity, aligns actions, and guarantees that collaboration abounds.

Guiding Questions
To bolster thinking using the Protecting Mindset, consider the following questions:

Culture and Talent Questions

- *Do we live our identity and maintain our esprit de corps?*
  - Developing a sense of purpose and community spurs productivity. Culture must be nourished, or entropy steals in, and spirit evaporates.

- *Do our decisions, practices, and actions support a high-performing culture?*
  - The organization's vision, mission, and guiding principles steer activity at all levels. Potential diversions from bedrock principles require immediate intervention.

- *Are we recognizing and rewarding teamwork and cooperation?*
  - High-functioning teams—even those working remotely or communicating virtually—maximize productivity, innovation, engagement, and commitment. Without team recognition, performance slips, and internal competition thrives.

- *Do we respect and value differences?*
  - Diverse perspectives produce better decisions and avoid stumbling into action without recognizing potential ramifications. Valuing diversity can also help firms recruit and retain top talent.

- *Are we recruiting the right people for our culture and mission?*
  - Ensuring a fit between an applicant and the organization's culture prevents the high cost of a poor hire. But employing the right person does not mean hiring the same kind of person as those in the company. Lack of diversity creates group-think and blind spots.

- *Are we expanding our core competencies?*
  - Needed competencies shift with new strategies, customers, technologies, and markets. En-

suring up-to-date competencies prepares the organization for the future.

- *Are we effectively onboarding, coaching, and developing employees?*
    — Orientation programs, ongoing training, and coaching empower a talented, committed workforce.

- *Are development opportunities comprehensive and effective?*
    — Since business constantly changes, investment in human capital must be constant and effectively targeted.

- *Do we retain our key talent?*
    — Essential skills can be difficult to obtain and costly to replace. Retaining key talent provides a valuable edge. Your talent pipeline and succession plan deserve close scrutiny.

- *Is top management actively engaged in developing talent?*
    — High-level managers are frequently the best trainers, coaches, and mentors—assuming they continually polish their own skills and agree to serve.

Management Questions

- *Do employees support the organization's traditions, mission, values, and goals?*
    — Employees must understand and endorse the company's mission, market, strategy, and goals in their day-to-day interactions.

- *Is communication consistent with stated values, traditions, and expectations?*

- Walking the talk builds trust, respect, and dedication. Obscure directives, value breaches, and unreasonable mandates destroy commitment and initiative.

- *Are work practices fair and followed?*
  - When assignments, promotions, and recognition appear unfair, employees shift to doing what gets noticed rather than what needs to be done.

- *Do our employees have the autonomy they need to do their jobs?*
  - Micromanaging diminishes performance. Waiting for the boss to decide delays action and squashes initiative. Autonomy encourages engagement and creativity.

- *Are we managing conflict promptly and effectively?*
  - Tolerating personal, unit, or cross-functional conflict in the hope that it will be resolved permits issues to fester and expand. Confronting issues early reduces distractions and maintains a goal orientation.

- *Are resolution paths clear for handling questions and confusion?*
  - Getting prompt answers reduces confusion, saves time, and enhances productivity.

Organizations that acquire and retain the best and brightest retain their reputation and competitive advantage. No organization can rest on its laurels or tightly hold onto its past. Every culture must be agile due to incessant change. Determining what to alter and when to do it requires the use of the Challenging Mindset.

Challenging Mindset

"Those who look only to the past are certain to miss the future."

— *John F. Kennedy*

Only fifty-two on the 1955 Fortune 500 list appeared on it in 2019. Recognizing that even dominant companies falter, the Challenging Mindset accepts the need for continual renewal and employs a forward-focused perspective to reposition the organization for the future.

This Mindset looks for emerging trends and opportunities. Ambiguity, paradox, and complexity are chances for revitalization. Looking at the big picture stresses long-term opportunities over short-term wins. Combining trailblazing inquisitiveness with a long-term perspective, this point of view examines what can be altered, abandoned, introduced, or modified to secure a promising tomorrow.

The pay-me-now-or-pay-me-more-later mentality addresses impediments to prevent costly obstacles. Change and substantial risk-taking are necessary to prevent debilitating ossification. The discomfort and confusion associated with change become a reasonable price for sustainability.

The Challenging Mindset tests the viability of existing practices, assumptions, markets, and standards. It searches for opportunities, identifies potential partnerships, and devises business strategies to reenergize and reshape the organization for lasting gain. Rejecting the stay-the-course approach, it readily disrupts the status quo to introduce new opportunities, business models, alliances, and market niches. It recognizes the need to abandon outdated practices and product lines in order to introduce promising alternatives, markets, and beneficial alliances.

Davis Printing

Tom's decision to hold a strategic-planning session was driven by the Challenging Mindset. Seizing an opportunity, he invested in another press despite his initial reluctance to assume the risk. Likewise, the promise of a rewarding future propelled his acquisition of a small printing company.

Focal Points

Signs of a Challenging Mindset priority include:

- Recognizing outdated practices and assumptions

- Examining the big picture

- Scanning for new trends

- Championing strategic thinking and risk-taking

- Valuing cross-disciplinary critical thinking

- Questioning sacred cows

- Rewarding change and agility

- Identifying potential partners or alliances

The Challenging Mindset priority emerges when complacency crushes initiative and when fresh ideas are routinely rejected. Good-enough thinking must be cast aside for an organization to be relevant and harvest promising opportunities. Like a chess master, the Challenging

Mindset evaluates multiple moves and counter-moves to win the long game. At other times—quite unlike the chess master—this Mindset boldly sweeps aside the rules of the game and creates a different version. Whether methodical or daring, this outlook stirs thinking and encourages a broad view of the future.

Unfettered by precedent, the Challenging Mindset considers novel, overlooked, or once-unfashionable alternatives. It questions traditional thinking such as the premise that bigger firms are always better or that the first to market always attains an unbeatable advantage. Tesla's entry into the car market, the emergence of cryptocurrency, and second-to-market Amazon would not be dominating several industries if the first comer always enjoyed unbeatable precedence. Sometimes, what is old is true. Sometimes, what is old is outdated.

Guiding Questions

The following questions jump-start the use of the Challenging Mindset:

Strategy Questions

- *Are we effectively leveraging technology?*
  - Outdated systems remain in place due to comfort with legacy systems, resistance to learning new systems, and adoption of shortcuts that mask the need for upgrades.

- *Are we effectively balancing short- and long-term goals?*
  - Adopting a short-term focus conceals the need for change, just as a preoccupation with the long term imperils current viability.

- *Have we identified credible alliances or partnerships?*

- Alliances increase capacity, enlarge market scope, and expand resources.

• *Is critical thinking effective and rewarded?*

  — Too often we reward only those who success-fully fight fires and solve simple problems. We must also reward critical thinking to guaran-tee that opportunities and risks are effectively vetted.

• *Do we systematically examine our successes and mistakes?*

  — After-action reviews provide insights. Fre-quently, we can learn more from missteps than from successful ventures.

• *Are we planning for our future?*

  — This question jolts thinking and encourages consideration of a wide range of opportunities.

Mental-Agility Questions

• *Can we identify and seize opportunities?*

  — Leaping forward is daunting but essential. When the pace of change is accelerating, orga-nizations need to discover opportunities.

• *Are we revising our policies and systems to meet emerging needs?*

  — Systems must be reconfigured to support evolving strategies and business models. Out-dated metrics and reward systems derail trans-formation.

• *Are we institutionalizing best practices?*

  — Recognizing best practices is not enough; they have to be spread across the organization.

- *Are we rewarding critical thinking and change management?*
  - Regularly rejecting novel ideas squashes engagement, creative thinking, and individual initiative.

- *Is it safe to be a devil's advocate?*
  - If challenging an idea results in shunning or disapproval, everyone will keep their head down and do what they have always done.

- *What will make us more agile and change ready?*
  - Asking questions, encouraging initiative, rewarding change advocates, and encouraging comprehensive analysis sustain a change-ready culture.

- *Is conformity or group-think concealing opportunities?*
  - The culture must support the expression of creative ideas, suggestions, and opportunities to prevent a go-along-to-get-along mentality.

Environment Questions

- *Do we regularly examine practices and test assumptions?*
  - If not, we cannot identify emerging trends and adapt to them quickly.

- *Do we understand environmental trends?*
  - We need to be aware of trends, but understanding their implications requires careful analysis, insight, and planning.

- *Are we monitoring nontraditional as well as traditional threats?*

  — Monitoring systems must detect unconventional as well as known risks. After all, paradigm-changing threats can arise from unexpected sources.

Adopting the Challenging Mindset means questioning long-standing and outdated practices and studying trends to discover emerging opportunities. After employing this macro-view, the next pressing concern centers on what new products or services are necessary to implement the renewal strategy. So, attention shifts back to the Inventing Mindset, where those novel opportunities become tangible offerings, and the cycle continues.

The Mindset cycle is predictable, but it is not automatic. Economic disruptions, international tensions, and governmental regulations can interrupt the cycle. Mindsets swing to target what matters most at a point in time. While we can predict certain changes, progress is not guaranteed.

13

Leveraging the Power of Mindsets

"Don't fight forces, use them."
— *R. Buckminster Fuller*

The *Merriam-Webster Dictionary* defines *lever* as "an inducing or compelling force."[1] The practice of Situational Mindsets is just such a tool. By unveiling fresh insights and opportunities, improving influence, and deterring conflict, it unlocks tremendous possibilities. At the same time, it exposes risks, unintended consequences, and implementation hurdles, thereby preventing domino-effect damage.

Like a kaleidoscope, where one small adjustment creates dramatic change, Mindsets paints a multifaceted picture of our current realities. Armed with the viewpoints of these six unique Mindsets, we can build bridges and teamwork to maximize engagement and results.

Influence

------

*"If there is any one secret of success, it lies in the
ability to get the other person's point of view
and see things from that person's angle as well
as from your own."*

— Henry Ford

The word *influencer* was coined to single out those with a track record of being persuasive. That term applies to those on social networks, but it also means those who coax or charm others, those who force others to accept a decision, and those who develop an agreement by examining options that gain active support. Only the last definition—a mutually satisfactory agreement—delivers lasting support. The others, at best, generate fleeting acceptance or reluctant compliance. When arm-twisting ends or when a wheedled agreement is exposed, cooperation evaporates.

Priority Analysis
We have all used the phrase "a penny for your thoughts," recognizing that current thinking steers decisions and actions. Situational Mindsets decodes which priority we are dealing with. Exchanging perspectives and exploring facts alter thinking without force or manipulation.

In the US, conversation often resembles a competitive sport. The first person who stops to take a breath feels as though the other has won the airtime battle. This stems from the assumption that if a person speaks long enough, repeats often enough, and asserts a perspective vigorously enough, that viewpoint will win. This is false. Some see probing and listening as inferior, deferential, or time-consuming. However, these provide lasting value since they reveal hot buttons, pinpoint concerns, and create a basis for discussion, as Brian discovered at Davis Printing. When he started questioning and listening, he learned what was driving his clients and how to serve them.

Open-Ended Questions

Open-ended statements and questions reveal information and build rapport. In *How to Talk to Practically Anyone about Practically Anything*, famed TV interviewer Barbara Walters revealed that she only had to offer one statement to start an interview: "Tell me about yourself."[2] This invariably elicited a wealth of knowledge and established rapport. In business, we can modify this powerful request by asking, "Tell me what you're working on," canceling the need to guess or presume what drives another person. Effective questions include:

- What goals are you focusing on now?

- What challenges are you confronting?

- What is critical or pressing right now?

- What risks are on the horizon?

- What keeps you awake at night?

Such open-ended and open-minded questions provide insight into another's immediate priorities, without having to be a Sherlock Holmes or psychoanalyst.

By listening, we can quickly grasp another person's Mindset and initiate a search for areas of agreement. For example, if a colleague is targeting product quality or meeting delivery schedules, the Performing Mindset is

the current priority. However, if the person is functioning from a different Mindset, we should adopt an approach targeting that Mindset.

Questions are key in revealing pressing concerns.
Typically, one or two priorities drive decision makers.
Our research at Enterprise Management Ltd. discovered
that 45 percent of respondents operated from one Situational Mindset, 31 percent employed two, and 22 percent
worked with three. Therefore, 98 percent of our database
had chosen a priority.[3] If nearly everyone has a Mindset priority, we should determine what that is because
working with priorities creates a productive, fact-based
exchange.

Priority-based questions demonstrate respect, display openness, and build relationships. Linkages are
created by commonality—athletes playing on the same
team, overseas tourists coming upon a citizen from their
own country, strangers coping with shared events such
as a hurricane. A willingness to listen creates a bond too.
Without such a link, conversations vacillate between ignoring other parties and competing with them.

Listening creates understanding. This chapter's
opening quote from Henry Ford is reinforced in *To Kill a
Mockingbird.* Atticus Finch counsels his daughter, Scout:
"You never really understand a person until you consider things from his point of view ... until you climb into
his skin and walk around in it."[4] Walking in another's
shoes—or skin—discloses insights into that person's
goals and diminishes defensiveness and disengagement.

Observations

In some instances, we may not be able to ask questions.
However, we can always listen, observe, and analyze
comments for pressing priorities. The statements below
reflect clues to particular driving Mindsets:

Inventing Mindset

- We must update our products to remain an industry leader.

- We need to discover unique ways to use the latest technology.

- Innovation is essential for our success.

Catalyzing Mindset

- Our success depends on responding swiftly to our customers' needs.

- We have to ensure customer satisfaction and listen to emerging requirements.

- We can retain our key customers through outstanding service.

Developing Mindset

- Our systems and policies need to match our strategies and goals.

- We need seamless execution and cross-functional collaboration.

- Our structure must facilitate information flow and effective decision-making.

Performing Mindset

- Identifying and removing bottlenecks improve productivity.

- Continuous improvement of quality and standards is essential to our success.

- We have to find ways to reduce costs and improve the bottom line.

Protecting Mindset

- We must keep our employees' competencies up-to-date.

- If we engage our employees and live our mission, we will retain our key talent.

- Succession planning guarantees a strong talent pipeline.

Challenging Mindset

- We need to validate and update our business model for our future success.

- Monitoring emerging trends will reveal promising opportunities for us.

- As we plan for the future, we should consider potential alliances and partnerships.

After we identify a person's Situational Mindset, we can adjust to ensure a mutually beneficial conversation.

Influencing without Authority

Everyone has influence, even without formal authority. Influence is a practice that entails seven steps:

1. *Identify the other party's current Mindset to prepare for the discussion.*

A person's Mindset may override a strictly logical approach because decision priorities merge experience and expectations with data. Understanding your audience's Mindset determines how to open a conversation. Jumping in and hoping your point of view will prevail are tempting, but the gamble may be costly. First impressions count, so starting out right is critical.

Knowing the existing Mindset priority permits you to start a conversation with a WIIFT (what's in it for them) approach. In the case of the Performing Mindset, an opening might address logistical difficulties or quality disparities, for example.

Attention to someone's interests generates a reciprocal response where the other person inquires into your priorities, and that build cooperation and respect.

2. Introduce your must-have goals.

After discussing the other person's issues, the next step is to explore the WIIFM (what's in it for me) issues. And here a caution is in order. You have to target the must-have outcomes rather than wished-for outcomes. Attempting to accomplish everything in one fell swoop is foolhardy. It is like a batter whose team needs a bunt or walk to win the game, but the batter gambles by swinging for the fences, hoping for a heroic game-ending home run. You are wiser to attain what you need now instead of hoping for a massive victory.

3. Identify multiple alternatives.

Next, search for traditional and nontraditional alternatives. To move the conversation beyond eitheror thinking, revisit the topic's parameters, generate alternatives, envision new synergies, alter the scope, investigate pilot options, and agree to work until there is a mutually beneficial plan.

Situational Mindsets expands the range of alternatives to uncover multiple solutions. It is estimated that ninety-five percent of the time there more than two options exist. Find them. This step rejects binary thinking, pressure for urgent agreement, and acceptance of implied constraints.

Kate used this process in her discussions with Tom. In preparation for this step, she had used his interest in increased sales and cost containment, then concentrated on her must-have request for CRM software. She considered multiple alternatives, from an outright software purchase to a subscription and a trial period. She presented the trial, conscious of his reluctance to invest and his ability to cancel the project if it did not prove its value.

By focusing on clear mutual gain, Kate bolstered her credibility and her status as a team player. Her attention to Tom's priorities avoided any appearance of being brash or self-serving, while also delivering a tool to help Sales.

This example captures how one person crafted a win-win outcome at the outset, but offering a solution at the start is not essential. In fact, jointly generating alternatives builds ownership and a spirit of collaboration. The following Mindset questions advance the search for mutually satisfactory actions:

- **Inventing:** Where do you think we should focus our innovative efforts?

- **Catalyzing:** Since our customers are key, how can we better serve them?

- **Developing:** What changes in policies, structure, or systems will create seamless operations.

- **Performing:** What can we do to improve productivity, workflow, or ROI?

- **Protecting:** Our workforce is vital to our future. How can we develop and retain our talent?

- **Challenging:** What emerging trends, risks, and opportunities should we evaluate?

In addition to the targeted Mindset questions above, the following general questions also exposes priorities:

186

- What options can we identify?

- What additional actions should we consider?

- What do you think is the most pressing issue?

- If we reconsidered timelines, resources, and other constraints, what alternatives could we discover?

- What can we learn from our customers, our competition, and our past experience to prepare us for future success?

- Who should we consult or get input from as we explore various initiatives?

- If we changed our discussion's scope or specifications, what options would surface?

- What existing assumptions should we reexamine?

These questions shift the focus from simple, fast resolutions to uncovering new synergies, solutions, and initiatives. They avoid being hemmed in by two choices, one that is feasible and a contrived option that is clearly unacceptable.

Numerous alternatives also prevent a split-the-decision-down-the-middle response that produces mutually unacceptable decisions. Those types of settlements generate buyer's remorse, in which both parties assume they should have gained more.

Attempting to launch a highly creative, untested solution without rigorous vetting is dangerous as well. Supposed slam dunks conceal danger in the short or long term. Take time to study the impact and ramifications carefully. Some supporters become infatuated with a dazzling idea; however, success is not measured by the wattage of the idea but by results. A less innovative plan that gains active support and can be implemented beats an impractical concept with limited backing.

4. Evaluate risks and projected impact.

Assess the feasibility of potential solutions. Evaluation factors might include resource requirements, degree of change, available personnel, legal ramifications, long-term costs, opportunity costs, and impact on the brand. Brian and Kate's revised First Light Stores proposal with guaranteed delivery times would work only if Production agreed to an aggressive schedule. Production had to be on board, or the customer would have been disappointed, and the guarantee would have been costly.

Brilliant ideas capture attention and stir enthusiasm, but Newton's third law of motion reminds us that for every action, there is an equal and opposite reaction. This means that for every new plan, ramifications must be weighed before we rush into action. One of the benefits of using Situational Mindsets is that it thwarts tunnel vision, offering the proverbial ounce of prevention to avoid paying the expensive pound of cure. Mindsets balances short- and long-term considerations and evaluates systems implications and risks.

5. Agree on a mutually acceptable plan.

Confirm that the proposed plan or decision captures a true meeting of the minds. Committing to a plan is quite different from merely complying with one. Separating the evaluation in the fourth step from the decision-making process in this step may seem insignificant, but combining these two steps shortchanges analysis and planning in favor of action. Step five ensures that everyone understands what is planned and gives their full support to the initiative.

6. *Develop and communicate the plan.*

When a plan impacts others, established practices, or ex-isting systems, this step is essential. In these instances, you need to obtain acceptance from implementers. This requires detailed execution planning since the workabil-ity of the plan, rather than its generalities, will win sup-port. Two-way discussion of the plan's nuts and bolts satisfies those who will be on the front line and prevents frustration and confusion.

7. *Monitor, adjust when warranted, and celebrate progress.*

No matter the decision's scope, the final influencing step emphasizes monitoring and adjusting during implemen-tation. Mid-course corrections are always needed. Apollo rockets were off course 97 percent of the time, but they still reached their destinations and returned to earth as a result of timely modifications.[5] Although organizational plans will probably remain on trajectory more often than space flight, fluctuations occur, and alterations main-tain progress. Attention typically centers on the plan's launch, but we must also give consideration to milestone progress. And progress deserves to be celebrated because that recognizes contributors and cements confidence in the change process.

Situational Mindsets and Change

"What gets us into trouble is not what we don't know.
It is what we know for sure that just ain't so."
— Unknown

Reflect on your last two or three change initiatives. Were they entirely successful, partially successful, or did they miss the mark? If they were not fully successful, do not be surprised. Research finds that the success rate of modification efforts varies between 9 and 30 percent.[6] Not great odds. Most are silently abandoned, significantly revised, or outright canceled, resulting in finger-pointing, frustration, and disappointment. To improve this dismal record, our approach to change must change. We have to be willing to clarify benefits from all viewpoints to gain commitments from others. And we need to regularly communicate, recognize progress, and commend the people who are making that progress possible.

Making Change Stick

Change is inevitable, but its acceptance is not. Since uncertainty, fear, and anxiety abound with new situations or procedures, resistance and foot-dragging blossom. Barebone summaries and taglines cannot extinguish worry. Silence, apathy, and anger signal the need for additional information, analysis, and modification. Taking the time to fully flesh out a plan saves time in the long run. Limited participation, apathy, and compliance indicate trouble during a shift, just as warning lights or strange noises under a car's hood indicate impending difficulties.

Converting go-along-to-get-along passive responses into active commitment pays off. Dedicated supporters, or change advocates, regularly go above and beyond expectations to reach goals. Converting a salute-and-execute mentality into enthusiastic approval requires presenting compelling benefits that resonate with individuals. The only change we can count on to garner fast support is an unexpected pay increase. Everyone immediately sees the benefit of more income. However, most initiatives will not gain immediate, full-hearted support, so communication through multiple channels is essential.

Communicating a change plan cannot rely on a single benefit. What one person considers desirable seems unwise or unimportant to others. An individual presently driven by the Challenging Mindset might support restructuring an organization to reduce the number of management levels, while a person with the Developing Mindset priority views the same proposal as disruptive, untested, unwarranted, and costly. These different perspectives can be bridged by highlighting how flatter organizations increase collaboration, improve decision-making speed, and enhance autonomy.

To make initiatives successful, benefits from all Mindsets must be identified and communicated.

Change Perspectives

The Situational Mindsets framework is depicted as a wheel reflecting their pattern. For instance, after a new product is developed using the Inventing Mindset, we have a strong tendency to next focus on customers. This portrayal also identifies two distinctive Mindset orientations to a proposed change.

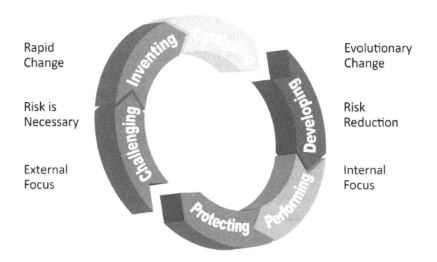

Rapid
Change

Risk is
Necessary

External
Focus

Evolutionary
Change

Risk
Reduction

Internal
Focus

The Situational Mindsets Wheel's right side, or hemisphere, consists of the Developing, Performing, and Protecting Mindsets, and these Mindsets seek incremental change based on internal data, with the goal of reducing risks. In contrast, the Challenging, Inventing, and Catalyzing Mindsets on the wheel's left hemisphere want fast change, employ external data, and tolerate risks as an acceptable cost for impressive rewards.

These opposite orientations can stir tension and promote stereotypes. The right-hemisphere Mindsets might label people using the left-hemisphere Mindsets as foolhardy and imprudent. Whereas, the left-hemisphere Mindsets might brand those using the right-hemisphere Mindsets as inflexible, resistant, and preferring the status quo.

To merge these hemisphere perspectives, we can listen to another's viewpoint and weigh the information driving that person's thinking and the benefits of that perspective. The left hemisphere contributes a sense of urgency, external awareness, creativity, and a willingness to transform to prepare for the future, while the right hemisphere's orientation offers careful internal analysis, potential barriers, cost-benefit analysis, and risk management for smooth execution.

Questions to blend and capture both change orientations include:

1. What critical issues confront us?

2. What systems or workforce issues might surface?

3. Do we have support from both decision makers and implementers?

4. What is the cost-benefit analysis?

5. How will this impact our customers and our brand?

6. What will position us for the future?

7. Does this change align with our culture, tradition, and mission?

8. What systems support, collaboration and resources are required?

9. Do we have the talent to implement the change?

10. Are the operating assumptions valid?

11. Will this initiative take resources away from other critical ventures?

12. When can we realistically expect results?

13. What is the worst and best case?

14. Have we checked in with all of our stakeholders?

15. How will this help our position in the industry?

These questions combine both perspectives and vet an initiative's viability. Asking the questions ensures a ready-aim-fire approach and avoids the left hemisphere's ready-fire tendencies or the right hemisphere's ready-aim-aim proclivities.

Bridging change perspectives builds goodwill, alignment, engagement, communication, trust, and respect. And it boosts the odds of success.

Situational Mindsets and Conflict

"In the middle of difficulty lies opportunity."
— Albert Einstein

Disagreements between Mindsets extend beyond change. Research shows that organizational conflict consumes at least 18% of a person's time[7] and results in an average decline of 25 percent in productivity for involved employees.[8] These statistics are significant whether the people are on the front line or in the executive suite. But the news is not all bad. Constructive tension advances innovation and productivity, but personal conflict breeds dysfunction, confusion, stubbornness, and inefficiency. Shrinking unproductive strife reduces stress, antagonism, and subpar performance.

Mindsets differ on what to fund, who to appoint, what actions to take when deliverables are due, and what goals to pursue. These differences can be settled by exchanging relevant facts and searching for alternatives. Concentrating on facts prevents being trapped by subjective influences on a person's agenda, character, or motivation. Fact-finding improves the prospect for lasting resolution. Research estimates these practices deliver a 6–9 percent reduction in the time consumed by conflict.[9] Translating that to hours, it means people gain ten to fourteen productive hours per month.

To keep things constructive, consider the following practices:

- Collect background information.

- Avoid jumping to premature conclusions.

- Demonstrate respect for the other person's Mindset.

- Separate the process of exploring ideas from the later process of making a decision.

- Separate facts from opinions and assumptions.

- Ensure everyone voices their issues and ideas.

- Collect information from others before leaders or influencers contribute.

- Use first names to smooth power differences.

- Summarize points made to ensure you have understood a perspective.

Devoting time and energy to listening and searching for mutually satisfying resolutions produce optimum results. Fiat, force and finger–pointing fail to subvert success.

Conflict Stages

Another way to deal with disagreements is to recognize how they progress through four stages. During the initial stage, the discussion centers on the wisdom of an action or idea. This issue prompts information exchange and critical analysis as springboards to understanding another's point of view. However, when understanding does not surface, tension enters the second stage, where the issue centers on what goals to pursue. The questions at this stage revolve around an objective analysis of each goals' necessity, results, urgency, benefit, cost, and impact. Both of these early stages concentrate on objective, discussable data and respect for another's point of view.

When differences over plans persist, and goals turn rigid, tension shifts into disruptive conflict. At this third stage, subjective aspects such as personality and motivation govern thinking, and positions harden. Respect diminishes, cooperation evaporates, and dysfunction surfaces. While we might invoke compromise, acquiescence, or arbitration, disputes can fester and toughen engendering negative stereotypes and animosity. Cliques form, rumors fly, falsehoods flourish, and productivity suffers. The conflict assumes a life of its own.

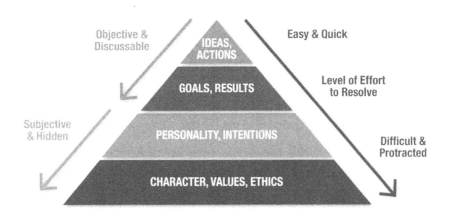

The image above displays the four stages and their key aspects. The first two stages—Ideas/Actions and Goals/Results—typically clear up quickly, creatively, and permanently. Resolving the last two—Personality/Intentions and Character/Values/Ethics—requires greater effort and time, reducing the likelihood of an agreement. With a subjective lens, resolution languishes, grudges develop, and distrust thrives.

Persistent conflicts rarely dissolve through the passage of time. The infamous Hatfield-and-McCoy feud lasted twenty-seven years, subsiding only after the conviction of eight Hatfields in 1890.[10] Resentments can simmer and resurface hotter than before at the slightest infraction.

At Davis Printing, the conflict between Sales and Production had escalated to stage four. Salespeople thought Production staff were obstructionists, and Production viewed Sales as having it easy. Kate and Richard defused these characterizations by sharing information, creating new procedures, and conferring with each other before making a decision that would impact the other's unit. The shift to interaction, transparency, and consultation transformed perceptions and increased cooperation.

Creating Common Ground

The Situational Mindsets Wheel displays the typical, comfortable Mindset progression. Uneasiness surfaces when the Mindsets are separated by one Mindset. And when they are opposite each other, tension is probable. Even with this divergence, connections remain and can transform the initial disparity into an agreement. The Mindset Wheel below identifies the connections between opposite Mindsets.

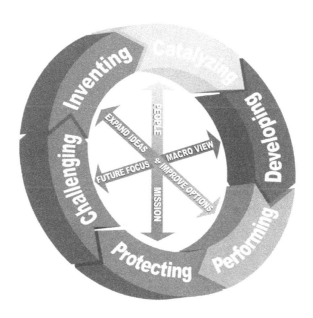

The Catalyzing and Protecting Mindsets differ over whether it is more important to serve external customers or prioritize internal staff and organizational culture. Despite focusing on distinct audiences, they have a common focus on people and mission fulfillment. Davis Printing's sales staff employed the Catalyzing Mindset's external focus, while Production's Performing Mindset priority concentrated on staffing and workload. By jointly reviewing special bid proposals, outsourcing work to reduce burnout, improving on-time deliveries, and recognizing how each unit contributed to turning the business around, both Mindsets' goals were fulfilled.

Potential discord between Inventing and Performing Mindsets revolve around the split between prioritizing innovation, new products, and inventive synergies versus the need to fine-tune existing processes and practices to maximize quality and ROI. Nonetheless, they share a desire for improvement. Tom's Performing Mindset prioritized raising profitability, while Kate used an Inventing Mindset as she targeted better technology and practices. Based on his concerns about overhead costs, she bridged the two Mindsets by pitching the CRM system as a cost-conscious tweak rather than a momentous leap.

The Developing and Challenging Mindsets spar over whether an internal or external macro-outlook should take precedence. Those operating from the Challenging Mindset seek new business models and niches, restructuring, and alliances. But venturing into uncharted territory clashes with the Developing Mindset's preference for proven, robust systems, vetted policies, established structure, and specified accountabilities. Tom's thinking eventually balanced these two Mindsets. His original focus on internal issues reduced his attention to strategic opportunities. However, after customer complaints decreased, collaboration increased, and sales rose, he shifted from his internal Developing Mindset to the Challenging Mindset's concentration on external opportunities. And with such a large shift, he recognized that his priorities had evolved.

Remaining objective, open, and resourceful resolves tension and conflict. One tool to keep our minds open to resolving perceived irreconcilable viewpoints is exploring an issue from all perspectives. This fosters alignment, acceptance, and commitment.

Situational Mindsets
Checklist

*"If you do not know how to ask the right
question, you discover nothing."*
— **W. Edwards Deming**

Many professions value inquiry. Journalists use the five
*W*s and one *H* (what, where, why, when, who, and how),
doctors learn medical triage protocols and use surgical
checklists, pilots employ preflight checklists, and law-
yers have standard systems to collect data from clients.
These tools and practices ensure that relevant factors
surface, avoiding omissions and miscalculation before a
decision is reached.

Centuries after Socrates demonstrated the power of
asking questions, we remain overly focused on training
individuals to find the right answer rather than also ad-
vancing the ability to ask the right questions. This oversight is glaring. Everyone benefits from effective inquiry
when confronting complex situations.

Given the complexity we face today, we need a checklist to ensure that all key areas are covered. Asking the
right questions spurs critical thinking, reveals potential
blind spots, improves productivity, builds engagement,
fosters collaboration, and manages risk.

Today, questioning remains essential to strategic, critical, and innovative thinking. Challenging long–standing

assumptions, encouraging critical analysis, and recognizing patterns are essential. However, valuing the process does not guarantee the practice or elicit eureka insights. The Situational Mindsets Checklist offers a tool for leaders, coaches, and mentors to capture current realities from every angle. It advances situational awareness and mental agility.

The following Mindsets checklist can easily be tailored to a specific industry, customer base, project, specialty, or organizational level:

Inventing Mindset

- What alternatives do we have?

- What outside-the-box thinking can we tap?

- What have we never tried before?

- If there were no barriers or constraints, what could we do?

- What is the ideal product or service?

- How can we take our existing products/services to a new level?

- What can we combine, remove, or alter to improve internal synergies?

- What can we gain from applying additional technology?

Catalyzing Mindset

- What will grow our customer base?

- What will keep us ahead of the competition?

- Do we collect customer feedback and use it appropriately?

- What will boost our brand?

- How are customer requirements changing?
- How can we improve our customer service?
- How can we respond more effectively to customer requests?
- Are we retaining our key customers?

Developing Mindset

- What are our goals?
- What is the best organizational structure?
- What will promote communication and timely decision-making?
- What systems do we need improve or realign?
- Are we effectively monitoring progress?
- Do we have the right balance between autonomy/delegation and control?
- What types of teams do we need?
- What will ensure smooth, silo-free execution?

Performing Mindset

- Is our cost-benefit analysis effective?
- What will improve operations and minimize deviations?
- What will remove bottlenecks and improve work-flow?
- What will reduce costs or improve productivity?
- What will keep production on time and on budget?
- What will boost our profit margins and ROI?
- What will improve quality?
- Where can we improve our supply chain?

Protecting Mindset

- What will support our culture and our values?
- Do we have the right staff with the right skill sets?
- What will sustain our commitment to fair and ethical practices?
- What will boost engagement?
- Are rewards/recognition aligned and effective?
- How can we develop future leaders?
- Is our succession plan effective?
- What will ensure a change-ready, engaged culture?

Challenging Mindset

- Are our assumptions valid?
- What emerging trends might impact us?
- Are we effectively balancing short- and long-term goals?
- What best practices should we institutionalize?
- Are there new business plans or models we should consider?
- What non-traditional risks are on the horizon?
- What alliances or partnerships are possible?
- Is strategic thinking practiced across the organization?

Conclusion

We live in an era dominated by change, complexity, and ambiguity. We cannot remain glued to our past if we want an impressive future. It is imperative to mine data, understand current realities, decipher nuances, recognize interdependencies, challenge cursory responses, identify patterns, and identify creative alternatives.

We must also move beyond the traditional two options. While some may identify a glass that is partially filled as half-empty, others see it as half-full. But we may also realistically conclude that someone has used the wrong size glass. Commitment to finding more options is critical to thriving in a rapidly changing environment.

The practice of Situational Mindsets reveals our realities, fosters engagement, circumvents risks, and seizes opportunities. We cannot do everything that we would like to do, but we can target what is vital at this moment to secure our success.

Notes

Introduction

Epigraph: Abraham Lincoln, Annual Message to Congress, December 1, 1862, Collected Works of Abraham Lincoln, vol. 5, p. 537, University of Michigan Digital Library Text Collections, https://quod.lib.umich.edu/l/lincoln/lincoln5/1:1126.1?rgn=div2;singlegenre=All;sort=occur;subview=detail;type=simple;view=fulltext;q1=act+anew#hl1.

1. Gurumurthy Kalyanaram and Ragu Gurumurthy, "Market Entry Strategies: Pioneers Versus Late Arrivals," strategy+business, July 1, 1998, https://www.strategy-business.com/article/18881?gko=64116.

2. Nelson Cowan, "Working Memory Maturation: Can We Get At the Essence of Cognitive Growth?" *Perspectives on psychological science: a journal of the Association for Psychological Science*, 11, no. 2 (2016): 239-64, https://www.ncbi.nlm.nih.gov/pmc/articles/PMC4800832/.

3. Joel Hruska, "Downed 737 MAX 8sLacked Safety Features Boeing Only Sells as Extras," ExtremeTech, March, 21, 2019, https://www.extremetech.com/extreme/288099-downed-787-max-8s-lacked-safety-features-boeing-only-sells-as-extras.

4. Chris Isidore, "Grounding all 737 Max planes could cost Boeing billions of dollars," CNN Digital, March 13, 2019, https://www.cnn.com/2019/03/13/investing/boeing-max-737-grounding/index.html.

Chapter 4

1. Arthur Miller Quotes, Goodreads, accessed August 19, 2019, https://www.goodreads.com/quotes/7175586-he-s-a-man-way-out-there-in-the-blue-riding.

Chapter 5

1. George S. Patton Quotes, BrainyQuote, accessed August 20, 2019, https://www.brainyquote.com/quotes/george_s_patton_130444.

Chapter 7

1. Quote Investigator, "The Customer Is Not an Interruption in Our Work; He Is the Purpose of It," August 2, 2012, https://quoteinvestigator.com/2012/08/02/gandhi-customer/.

2. Quote Investigator, "May You Live in Interesting Times," December 18, 2015, https://quoteinvestigator.com/2015/12/18/live/.

Chapter 11

Epigraph: A Quote By Dalai Lama XIV, Goodreads, accessed August 14, 2019, https://www.goodreads.com/quotes/7062036-when-you-talk-you-are-only-repeating-what-you-already.

1. Wayne Gretzky Quotes, BrainyQuote, accessed August 14, 2019, https://www.brainyquote.com/quotes/wayne_gretzky_383282.

2. Tim Fenster, "Misidentification Common in Wrongful Arrests," *Lockport Union-Sun & Journal*, July 23, 2018, https://www.lockportjournal.com/news/local_news/misidentification-common-in-wrongful-arrests/article_4f534b30-c8be-5d29-8ad0-d2208663ec78.html.

3. "What Role Did Securitization Play in the U.S. Subprime Mortgage Crisis?" Investopedia, last modified July 15, 2019, https://www.investopedia.com/ask/answers/041515/what-role-did-securitization-play-us-subprime-mortgage-crisis.asp.

4. Samuel Bacharach, "Leadership Without Presumption: Lessons From Eisenhower," *Inc.*, June 26, 2013, https://www.inc.com/samuel-bacharach/leadership-without-presumption-lessons-from-eisenhower.html.

5. Dwight D. Eisenhower Quotes, BrainyQuote, accessed August 16, 2019, https://www.brainyquote.com/quotes/dwight_d_eisenhower_135290.

Chapter 12

Epigraph: Lucius Annaeus Seneca Quotes, BrainyQuote, accessed August 15, 2019, https://www.brainyquote.com/quotes/lucius_annaeus_seneca_100585.

Inventing Mindset Epigraph: Benjamin Franklin Quotes, Goodreads, accessed August 14, 2019, https://www.goodreads.com/quotes/55530-to-cease-to-think-creatively-is-to-cease-to-live.

1. Steven Tweedie, "The 14 Best Steve Jobs Quotes to Inspire Your Inner Creative Genius," *Inc.*, July 13, 2015, https://www.inc.com/business-insider/14-most-inspiring-steve-jobs-quotes.html.

2. Nathan Furr, "How Failure Taught Edison to Repeatedly Innovate," *Forbes*, June 9, 2011, https://www.forbes.com/sites/nathanfurr/2011/06/09/how-failure-taught-edison-to-repeatedly-innovate/#26e53c0965e9.

Catalyzing Mindset Epigraph: Wikipedia, s.v. "The customer is always right," last modified May 2, 2019, 22:25, https://en.wikipedia.org/wiki/The_customer_is_always_right.

3. Quote Investigator, "It's Easier to Ask Forgiveness Than to Get Permission," June 19, 2018, https://quoteinvestigator.com/2018/06/19/forgive/.

Developing Mindset Epigraph: Henry David Thoreau Quotes, *Walden*, Goodreads, accessed August 14, 2019, https://www.goodreads.com/quotes/3234-if-you-have-built-castles-in-the-air-your-work.

4. Davis Balestracci, "No Wonder Executives Hated Deming," Quality Digest, July 30, 2012, https://www.qualitydigest.com/inside/quality-insider-article/no-wonder-executives-hated-deming.html.

Performing Mindset Epigraph: Ralph S. Larsen, quoted in Larry Bossidy and Ram Charan, *Execution: The Discipline of Getting Things Done* (New York: Crown Business, 2002).

5. Peter Drucker Quotes, AZquotes, accessed August 16, 2019, https://www.azquotes.com/author/4147-Peter_ Drucker.

Protecting Mindset Epigraph: John Wooden Quotes, AZquotes, accessed August 14, 2019, https://www. azquotes.com/quote/549461.

Challenging Mindset Epigraph: John F. Kennedy, "Remarks of the President in the Assembly Hall of Paulskirche, Frankfurt, Germany, 25 June 1963," folder: Address in the Assembly Hall at the Paulskirche, Frankfurt, 25 June 1963, Archives, John F. Kennedy Presidential Library and Museum, https://www.jfklibrary.org/asset-viewer/archives/JFKPOF/045/JFKPOF-045-023.

Chapter 13

Epigraph: R. Buckminster Fuller Quotes, BrainyQuote, accessed August 15, 2019, https://www.brainyquote.com/ quotes/r_buckminster_fuller_151687.

1. Merriam-Webster, s.v. "lever (n.)," accessed August 16, 2019, https://www.merriam-webster.com/dictionary/ lever.

Influence Epigraph: Henry Ford Quotes, BrainyQuote, accessed August 15, 2019, https://www.brainyquote. com/quotes/henry_ford_400461.

2. Barbara Walters and June Callwood, *How to Talk to Practically Anyone about Practically Anything* (New York: Dell Publishing Company, 1979).

3. Mary Lippitt, *Brilliant or Blunder: 6 Ways Leaders Navigate Uncertainty, Opportunity, and Complexity* (Enterprise Management Ltd., 2014).

4. Harper Lee, *To Kill a Mockingbird* (New York: Warner Books, 1960).

5. Paul Saffo, "We were off-course 97% of the time," comment on NavList quoting a "NASA old-timer," June 11, 2016, http://fer3.com/arc/m2.aspx/We-were-offcourse-97-time-PaulSaffo-jun-2016-g35557.

Situational Mindsets and Change Epigraph: Though many attribute this quotation to Mark Twain, see: Quote Investigator, "It Ain't What You Don't Know That Gets You Into Trouble. It's What You Know for Sure That Just Ain't So," November 18, 2018, https://quoteinvestigator. com/2018/11/18/know-trouble/.

6. John P. Kotter, *Leading Change* (Boston: Harvard Business School Press, 1996).

Situational Mindsets and Conflict Epigraph: Albert Einstein Quotes, Goodreads, accessed August 15, 2019, https://www.goodreads.com/quotes/7275-in-the-middle-of-difficulty-lies-opportunity.

7. Barbara J. Kreisman, Insights into Employee Motivation, Commitment, and Retention, PhD Research/White Paper, Insights Denver (Denver: Business Training Experts, 2002).

8. Deborah Mihm and Matt Fairbank, *Workplace Conflict and Your Business*, Appendix, Item A (Yakima, Washington: Dispute Resolution Center of Yakima and Kittitas Counties, 2012) https://c.ymcdn.com/sites/nafcm.site-ym. com/resource/resmgr/Research/Workplace_Conflict_ and_Your_.pdf.

9. Mihm and Fairbank, *Workplace Conflict*.

10. Wikipedia, s.v. "Hatfield–McCoy Feud," last modified August 13, 2019, https://en.wikipedia.org/wiki/Hatfield–McCoy_feud#Trial.

Situational Mindsets Checklist Epigraph: W. Edwards Deming Quotes, BrainyQuote, accessed August 15, 2019, https://www.brainyquote.com/quotes/w_edwards_ deming_384036.

Acknowledgments

It is my pleasure to recognize many of the creative minds that have contributed to this book creation and completion. I want to thank David Covey encouraged me to write this book, and I deeply appreciate his support and friendship.

I am delighted to give special attention to my editor Irene Chambers. And also to Alan Axelrod for his sharp eye and indispensable advice. Special recognition also goes to Maggie Wheeler for sharing her vast experience, Dorren MacAulay for our research, Sara Berglund for her creativity, Andy Meaden for the cover art, and Jane Anderson and Laura Barclay for their guidance.

I am also thankful that Virginia Bianco Mathis, Dan Gerson, Paula Moreno, Wendy Gourley, and Brian Schwartz who offered their wisdom and support.

Consulting and coaching clients, program participants, and graduate students are too numerous to mention, but be assured that I am deeply indebted to you all. Special thanks go to those who contributed by granting interviews and sharing their experience. This book insufficiently captures their impressive wealth of experience.

A final note of appreciation to family and friends who support and celebrated milestones with me.

— Mary Lippitt

About the Author

Dr. Mary Lippitt is an award-winning author, consultant and speaker targeting organizational results. For over 30 years, she has served major corporate and government clients in the US and abroad, including American Express, Bank of America, CSX, Florida Blue, Lockheed Martin, Marriott, the National Science Foundation, TRW, the US Department of Energy, and the US Marine Corps.

Her groundbreaking work on *Situational Mindsets* offers a no-nonsense checklist enabling leaders to successfully navigate change while avoiding pitfalls and delivering results.

Mary is a thought leader who founded Enterprise Management to stimulate systems thinking, boost leadership effectiveness, and elevate business acumen. The company assists leaders, teams, and organizations to develop business acumen, change management, strategic thinking and planning, mental agility, leadership development effectiveness, and critical thinking.

She has authored: *The Leadership Spectrum* (Bronze Award for Best Business Book of the Year, Foreword Magazine, 2002), *Discover Your Inner Strengths* (co-authored with K. Blanchard, S. Covey, and B. Tracey, 2009), *Brilliant or Blunder* (2014), and *Situational Mindsets: Targeting What Matters When It Matters* (2019). She is also researched and published the Situational Mindsets Indicator.

Her work has been featured in numerous publications, including the Huffington Post, OD Practitioner, BizCatalyst360, Executive Excellence, The Journal of Business Strategy, Industry Week, Association for Talent Development and Sirius Radio.

She has frequently served on numerous local, religious, and non-profit boards and established a scholarship program for children in the foster-care system.

Mary earned a Doctorate in Business Administration from Nova University and currently instructs MBA students at the University of South Florida. She lives in the Tampa Bay area, where her family likes to visit and where her orchids thrive.

You can connect with Dr. Lippitt at:
Email: *mary@situationalmindsets.com*
Linkedin: *https://www.linkedin.com/in/marylippitt/*
Twitter: *@marylippitt*
Website: *www.enterprisemgt.com*

About Enterprise
Management Limited

Enterprise Management helps leaders navigate dynamic changes and organizational paradoxes to deliver results. The firm offers training, consulting, speaking, and inventories focused on business outcomes.

Services and materials incorporating the Situational Mindset model include:

- *Situational Mindsets Indicator*® an inventory that examines a leader's or a team's current situational mindsets and potential blind spots for a specific initiative. It fosters mental agility and critical thinking.

- *Situational Mindsets Agility: Targeting What Matters* training program provides a road map for capturing situational insights and discovering new solutions.

- *Brilliant or Blunder Action Guide* book provides effective and, practical tools for deciphering priorities to leverage complexity and uncertainty.

- *Risk and Opportunity Practicum* training program develops program evaluation and analytical skills through a cohort model working on a change initiative for their unit.

- *Aligning for Success* program assesses an organization's current alignment by examining results and addresses what areas need attention to ensure long-term success.

Enterprise Management also offers customized programs, speaking engagements, and consulting using the Situational Mindsets and Aligning for Success framework.

Additional information can be found at:
www.enterprisemgt.com or contact Dr. Lippitt at *mary@situationalmindsets.com*